What's the Right Thing to Do?

What's the Right Thing to Do?

Promoting Thoughtful and Socially Responsible Behavior in the Early Childhood Years

Selma Wassermann

ROWMAN & LITTLEFIELD
Lanham • Boulder • New York • London

Published by Rowman & Littlefield
An imprint of The Rowman & Littlefield Publishing Group, Inc.
4501 Forbes Boulevard, Suite 200, Lanham, Maryland 20706
www.rowman.com

6 Tinworth Street, London SE11 5AL

Copyright © 2019 by Selma Wassermann

All rights reserved. No part of this book may be reproduced in any form or by any electronic or mechanical means, including information storage and retrieval systems, without written permission from the publisher, except by a reviewer who may quote passages in a review.

British Library Cataloguing in Publication Information Available

Library of Congress Cataloging-in-Publication Data

Names: Wassermann, Selma, author.
Title: What's the right thing to do?: promoting thoughtful and socially responsible behavior in early childhood years / Selma Wassermann.
Description: Lanham, Maryland : Rowman & Littlefield, 2019. | Includes bibliographical references and index.
Identifiers: LCCN 2019001383 | ISBN 9781475848564 (cloth) | ISBN 9781475848571 (pbk.) | ISBN 9781475848588 (electronic)
Subjects: LCSH: Moral education (Early childhood) | Early childhood education--Moral and ethical aspects. | Early childhood education--Social aspects. | Though and thinking--Study and teaching (Early childhood)
Classification: LCC LB1139.35.M67 W37 2019 | DDC 370.11/4--dc23
LC record available at https://loc.gov.2019001383

Contents

Preface		vii
Acknowledgments		xi
Introduction		1
1	It's a Dilemma!: Take That!	5
	Theoretical Foundations of Moral Behavior	6
2	Making Sense of a Complex World: What's the Right Thing to Do?	11
	What Can Teachers and Parents Do?	12
3	Children as Decision Makers	15
	Thinking and Deciding	17
	Some Caveats	17
	Freedom to Choose and Empowerment	19
4	Introduction to the World of Moral Dilemmas	21
	It's Complicated	21
	Adult-Child Discussions About Moral Issues	25
	The Value of Small-Group Work	27
5	Stories, Mini-Cases, Books, Films, and Classroom Incidents	29
	Mini-Cases	30
	What's a Case?	31
	Twenty-Two Mini-Cases	32
	Inviting Children's Stories About Their Own Dilemmas	46
	Children's Books and Stories	49
	Films	52
6	Putting Moral Behavior Into Action: A Chapter Primarily for Teachers	55
	Community Projects	56
	Extracting Meaning From Experience	62
	Journals	66
7	Discussion Strategies to Examine Moral Issues	69
	Learning Discussion Skills by Observing the "How" in Action	69
	The Interactive Dialogue	77
	The Teacher/Parent in the Process	81
	Nondefensive Awareness of Self	81

8	Even Children Can Make a Difference	83
	Children Who Make a Difference	84
	Conclusion	86

Bibliography	87
Index	89
About the Author	95

Preface

Ask anyone who has spent any time with young children. They will know that teachers' and parents' lives are riddled with decisions that would tax a Solomon. Some of those decisions are mundane. Others require wisdom and sensitivity that were never taught in school. If you wonder why parents and teachers are exhausted at the end of every day, try to envision the nature and quantity of the decisions that demand their immediate response.

"May I sharpen my pencil, Mrs. Jones?"

"Mom, Billy just peed his pants."

"Tamara took my book."

"But why?! Why should I have to do that?"

"Rosa pushed me and called me a bad name."

"I wanted to buy a cookie, but I lost my money."

"My dad hit my mother, and she cried."

"I saw Philip take Sonia's lunch."

"Daniel has a big hole in his pants."

"I don't want to play with him. He's stupid."

"He smells bad. I don't want to sit next to him."

The decisions that don't require a lot of weight can be tossed off without a second thought.

"May I sharpen my pencil?"

"Of course."

"Tamara took my book."

"I'll ask her to return it to you, Susie."

"I wanted to buy a cookie, but I lost my money."

"Not to worry, William. Here's another nickel."

And there are the decisions that try adults' souls and keep them up at night, worrying and wondering *if* that was the right choice and whether there will be unforeseen consequences of the decision.

In my 50+ years of classroom teaching, in the public schools and in the academy, I have made some values-related decisions that continue to haunt me even though I am now several years into retirement.

In a grade 6 class where my students were put to the task of evaluating their own work and filling in their own report cards (no kidding), Harold gave himself a grade of B in social studies. When he came up for a conference about his self-evaluation, I queried him about the grade he had given himself and asked how he could justify that, given that he had not completed any of his social studies work. His response was to tell me that if he took home any grade lower than a B, his dad would murder him. I allowed him the B. Was that the right thing to do?

In another grade 6 class, Gary, who struggled desperately in his academic work, kept turning in his math seatwork with at least 19 errors out of 20 examples, despite my giving him number facts that were more appropriate for the lower grades. Gary struggled with simple addition, and numbers seemed to defeat him. The price he was paying in his self-esteem was huge, and I cringed every time I marked his paper. No matter what strategy I used to help him count and compute, he was unable to achieve even a modest success.

In a move that I never learned in any education class or textbook, I took his math paper home, erased about eight of the wrong answers and filled in the correct ones. When I returned Gary's paper the next day, I told him that he had gotten 10 examples correct out of 15—a milestone! I never told that to a soul, but with those falsely elevated marks, Gary's role among his classmates as the "most stupid student in the class" began to shift. Was that the right thing to do?

The money we had been collecting in the grade 5 class to go on a field trip was taken from the bottom drawer of my desk, where I had kept it—without thought—for safekeeping. I suspected that Dennis, who had been in the room during lunch hour, had taken it. I told the class that the money had been stolen and that we were now unable to proceed with our plans to go on the trip. The children were shocked and angry. But I was adamant.

During the middle of the afternoon, Dennis and his buddy, Eddie, went to the boys' bathroom and came back with an envelope full of coins and dollar bills. "Here, Mrs. Wassermann. We found the money. It was hidden in the ceiling of the boys' bathroom." The children were elated, and Dennis and Eddie were heroes. In my heart, I suspected the real story but allowed the incident to pass, thanking Dennis and Eddie for finding the money. Was that the right thing to do?

I look back on those decisions I had made as a fledgling teacher and realize that my choices were influenced by what I considered to be important values that I wanted to protect. In the case of Harold, I wanted to protect him from losing his father's respect. In the case of Gary, I wanted to protect his very fragile self-esteem from yet another blow. In the case of Dennis, I wanted to protect the possibility that he might recognize that crime had some harsh consequences and that he might be reconsidering his actions.

Other adults might weigh all of these decisions differently—it all depends on what's important. What are the values that underlie one's choices, when and if the decisions to be made are value-laden? To be aware of that, I believe, helps to inform our choices. And when our values and the knowledge of what's important to us are clear and made with conscious awareness, the tough decisions we have to make are a bit clearer.

The book I have written is about enabling young children to come to sharper awareness of the values-laden decisions they make, because I believe that how and what we choose is a "tell" about who we are and what we stand for.

"Our decisions are us!" Sure, we toss off choices about matters of small consequence without a lot of thought. For if we had to think deeply and profoundly about everything, we'd be exhausted in the process. But when it comes to matters of significance, it behooves us to ask ourselves, What does this choice say about me as a person? What does it say about me to the world? What are the values I hold that led me to that choice?

Should such considerations about decision making be made in the early childhood years?

Given my own long-term experience working with children of all ages, I would say, unequivocally it is not too early to begin asking children even at age five about their values-related decisions, talking with them about why those decisions were made and what they see as some consequences of their choices. Allowing children choices and inviting thoughtful inquiry into those choices form the building blocks of socially responsible behavior—and the more this can be done in a climate of safety and respect for children and their choices, the more we can hope that our children will grow to become more thoughtful, more responsible, more caring adults.

So do the materials and teaching strategies contained in the subsequent chapters work for all children? Are they guarantees for every child in every situation?

Nothing I know of in the annals of child development is a 100% guarantee of what will work—and anyone who is silly enough to make that claim should be discredited. But given what David Brooks (2010) wrote, that "social norms fall on prepared ground; we come equipped to learn fairness and other virtues," there is a better than even chance that by exposing young children to many and frequent opportunities to make choices that are of consequence in their lives, and by asking them to reflect on those choices, in the presence of respect and in the absence of moral judgment, we have a good chance of helping our little ones become more thoughtful, more caring, more responsible citizens.

He was, even at age 11, what might be thought of as a "street tough"—leather jacket, torn jeans, boots—who was bragging about his best friend whose brother was now in reform school, and who himself was heading toward a life without adequate parental supervision. We had, each morning, a circle of those who wanted to participate—called a V-group—where the children could come and talk about issues in their lives that were puzzling or worrying. The plan was to see if some values-laden decisions could be brought under their scrutiny—in the absence of moral judgment from the teacher and with observable demonstration of respect for their choices.

It took a few months for him to own up to his action—the copping of a nail polish from Long's Drug Store in the strip mall—one that was urged by his mother. He was demonstrably uneasy about both his action and his confession. The other children gasped but remained quiet, waiting for me. I tucked in my "tsk tsk" and instead said, "You seem to be a little uncomfortable about having done that, Joe." He put his head down and said nothing more. It was the only time he volunteered to participate in the V-group. But I did learn that he had gotten the award for the "boy who had made the most progress" in his next year of school. Had that made a difference? I would love to believe it so. We teachers do like a happy ending.

Acknowledgments

My beloved great-grandchildren, Maya, Kai, and Ruben Maslow, to whom I look for wisdom about the lives of young children, are at the forefront of my mind as I write about moral development in young children. They are generous in giving me their ideas and in keeping me abreast of what goes on in their school and at-home lives, an abundance of data that informs my work. My family has been stalwart in supporting me and my work, and I am blessed with their love and their encouragement to keep writing. My esteemed colleagues, Jim Raths and Bill Cliett, took great pains to read and respond to earlier drafts and gave me feedback that guided further edits. I am grateful to them for taking the time to do that and giving me the benefit of their advice, as I am to my publisher, Tom Koerner, for his confidence in me and my work.

Introduction

Making choices is one of the more pervasive acts of life. Almost every action we take demands that choices be made. Knowing how to choose wisely, to choose after reflection, to be aware of what motivates the choice, to see the consequences of that choice on others enables us to live healthier, more productive, and more responsible lives. Sometimes, the burden of making difficult choices, of knowing "the right thing to do," is so confounding that we turn for advice to "agony aunts"—people who are paid to guide us to more moral and reasonable actions. And while their advice informs us, we are often still not sure whether taking it is the right thing to do.

There is now growing evidence that our values-related choices may have biological origins, but there is no doubt that the skills of making wise and informed decisions are cultivated with reflection on practice—repeated opportunities to choose, followed by critical analysis of how we came to those choices and what values we hold that have led us to those decisions. Given the moral challenges of our time, such decisions are harder to make, and the determination of what's the right thing to do has become increasingly complex. More than a few have questioned whether morality will be eclipsed by the contemporary challenges of social media, biotechnology, and artificial intelligence.

We now live in a world in which elected officials on whom we counted to be responsible leaders have revealed behavior that is morally repugnant. We've learned that among large corporations, executives have pursued greater profits at the expense of the general public. Our growing anxiety about climate change and its effect on our health and the future of the planet creates considerable tension about how to reconcile the goals of business with the general good. On a daily basis, in newspapers and on TV news, we read and hear stories about mendacity in public office, racial injustice, terrorism, changes in family structures, gender issues, immigration, and other equally compelling problems that defy simple solutions. With fewer moral exemplars and flawed role models, how are children to know what's right, good, decent, and socially responsible? "Do as I say, not as I do" is hardly a viable tenet to guide children's choices.

Important opportunities to develop more thoughtful and responsible decision-making behavior begin in the early childhood years. Growing independent, reasoned, and reasonable adults begins with allowing children, even young children, many opportunities to choose, to make choices that may be examined in the light of what it means to lead a good and responsible life. To that end, many schools have put new emphasis on social responsibility and character development in an attempt to help children at all ages grow with wisdom and maturity in their choices and actions. Morality, after all, is the opposite of unreasonableness, capriciousness, despotism, and tyranny.

Teachers, who have traditionally been responsible for developing children's academic skills, are now, along with parents and other caregivers, charged with promoting their thoughtful and socially responsible behavior. Both of these goals are now seen as high-priority educational concerns.

This book proceeds from the premise that the development of socially responsible behavior is a necessary educational goal that should sit side by side with academic achievement. The first chapters identify the need for building socially responsible behavior in the primary years and back this premise up with a supportive theoretical and research framework.

The succeeding chapters provide extensive examples of materials that teachers and parents may use to engage children in the examination of moral issues. These materials include brief stories, or *mini-cases*, each one focused on a particular dilemma related to the experiences of young children. The dilemmas presented avoid giving simplistic answers to complex problems. Instead, they seek to engage children in thoughtful consideration of alternatives, exploring different points of view and examining potential consequences to proposed actions. In short, they build children's intelligent habits of thinking—requiring them to think before they act, to examine data, to analyze data, to consider alternatives, and to suggest action, with a mind toward understanding implications and consequences.

Subsequent chapters are devoted to how teachers and parents may conduct adult-child discussions using reflective responses and higher-order questions, so that children may examine dilemmas in the absence of moral judgments. As children become more habituated to think before acting, to understand the values they hold that guide their actions, and how their actions bear on the health and safety of others, they become more self-aware and, thus, make fewer foolish choices. The importance of group work in classrooms as an adjunct to the examination of moral issues, the value of teaching as learning and of community involvement in civic projects, is also addressed.

A final chapter deals with how teachers and parents may assess the results of their efforts.

What's the Right Thing to Do? adds to the resources for teachers and parents in offering not principles of character development but important tools for carrying out effective teaching strategies that build caring environments in the classroom and home; tools for teaching children to weigh decisions in the face of potential consequences, examine rationales for their choices, and study the effects of their choices on others; tools for helping children to think more carefully about ethical problems by having them discuss dilemmas that arise frequently in school and at home, in the presence of the moral freedom to determine for themselves what it means to lead a good and virtuous life.

The vital link that this book adds to the discourse is the connection between thinking and decision making, since, as Derek Bok (2008) has written, "proficiency in critical thinking is a necessary condition for making thoughtful judgments about problems that lack definite answers."

ONE

It's a Dilemma!

Take That!

Walking was still a challenge for him, and it was sweet to watch him toddling across the room, trying hard to keep himself upright. The lab assistant helped him up onto a chair, and told him to watch the puppet show, which was about to begin. Riley, who was still preverbal, was just one year old, and while speech had yet to come to him, he did understand much of what he was told. He fixed his attention onto the stage, where the puppets were in place, ready to begin the show.

Two puppets, one dressed in green and one in blue, were playing ball, each catching and tossing the ball to each other. After about three or four tosses, the "green" puppet picked up the ball and ran offstage with it, leaving the "blue" puppet behind. Riley's attention was riveted to the scene, and then the curtain closed and both puppets were brought to the table where Riley sat.

On the table was a bowl of M&M's chocolate candies, and Riley was told that he could give some treats to the puppets. Riley gave one chocolate to the blue puppet that had been left behind but refused to give a candy to the green puppet who had made off with the ball. And in a more telling move, he smacked the green puppet on the head with his hand (Bloom, 2010).

From where does a one-year-old get his sense of morality? How did this little boy know that what the green puppet did was not right?

THEORETICAL FOUNDATIONS OF MORAL BEHAVIOR

The research and development of theory about morality in very young children has a long history. Nearly 40 years ago, George Pugh (1977) theorized that evolution's behavioral plan for the human species must be defined in an underlying system of values—an essential part of the human brain.

Richard Dawkins's landmark best seller, *The Selfish Gene* (1976) examined the biology of selfishness and altruism, concluding that "gene selfishness will usually give rise to selfishness in individual behavior; however, as we shall see, there are special circumstances in which a gene can achieve its own selfish goals best by fostering a limited form of altruism at the level of individual animals."

These early authors set the stage for the later examination of the relationship between genetic dispositions and moral behavior.

More recent theories stand in contradiction to the work of Jean Piaget (1932/1965), who in the 1930s offered his "stages of moral development," in which he suggested that premoral judgment, the first stage of human development, "lasts from about birth to about five years of age"—a time at which children "simply do not understand the concept of rules and have no idea of morality."

In making his determinations, Piaget presented young children with "moral dilemmas," each consisting of a pair of stories: In one, a child deliberately causes a small amount of damage; in the other, the damage caused was accidental but much greater. Piaget asked children which of the characters deserved to be punished the most and tried to find out not just their answers but the reasoning they used to arrive at them. According to Piaget, younger children focused more on consequences while older children also took intent into account.

Critics of Piaget's work found that replications of his studies did not lead to similar results. His questioning techniques also came under scrutiny due to their subtle leading children to specific answers. Additional criticism was made on the grounds that Piaget's moral "universals" were culture-specific, and that children in non-Western cultures would likely give different responses than the children in the Piaget sample.

On another dimension, Piaget's theory was criticized because of his view that "all morality comes from socialization"—a theoretical position that was later undermined by evolutionary psychology, which linked morality with genetic endowment. (Chandler, Greenspan, & Barenboim, 1973).

Lawrence Kohlberg (1981), a professor at Harvard University, carried out research in moral development at Harvard's Center for Moral Education in the 1970s. Following in the footsteps of Piaget, Kohlberg suggested that humans developed their moral reasoning in a series of stages, beginning at the elementary school level—the first stage, in which children behave as they are told to by some authority figure. Obedience is compelled by threat or punishment, and "good behavior" is characterized by acting in one's own best interests.

Kohlberg's view was that although most adults did not reach the highest level of moral functioning, moral development could better occur when people were presented with moral dilemmas that "would help them see the reasonableness of a higher stage of morality and encourage their development in that direction."

Criticisms of Kohlberg's work came from several sources. One suggested that he emphasized "justice" to the exclusion of other moral values. Another was that his "stages" created such an overlap that they were unable to be regarded as separate domains. A third was that the reasons he found for moral choices were mostly post hoc rationalizations by both decision makers and those researchers studying them. Moreover, critics pointed out that his presentation of moral dilemmas was not culturally neutral.

Carol Gilligan (1982), a colleague and critic of Kohlberg who was developing her own theoretical position about morality, indicated the need to examine differences in moral judgments not only in culture but in sex, social class, race, and ethnicity.

It is in Kohlberg's work, however, that can be found the first reference to the use of "moral dilemmas" as a means of promoting moral development in children, the use of the term *dilemmas* indicating that there is no superior outcome or judgment.

During the same decade as Kohlberg did his research, Louis Raths (1973) wrote his best-selling book about "values theory" in which he offered the hypothesis that "lack of clear values" resulted in certain observable and dysfunctional behaviors in children and that if teachers worked to enable children to "clarify" their beliefs and values, those dysfunctional behaviors would, over time, diminish.

Raths and Kohlberg were in agreement that there was an important relationship between the development of intelligence and the development of morality—that the stimulation of "active thinking" about moral issues and decisions was the basis for moral development. This was also borne out by the work of R. S. Peters (1970), who wrote that morality and moral judgments were a product of reason.

Raths, however, was among the first to identify how teachers might put these ideas to work in classrooms when he identified the various ways in which teachers could enable children to think more clearly about what they believed, what they cared about, what they prized, and what they were willing to affirm as those beliefs which they held dear (Raths, Harmin, & Simon, 1966/1978). Obviously, these suggestions apply to parents and other adults who are in positions of supervision of young children.

Following the publication of Raths's *Values and Teaching* (1966), there occurred wide and extensive "workshopping" in "values clarification" given by several of his graduate students—and perhaps the ways in which these workshops were conducted were what led to considerable criticism in the academy, which in turn did a great deal to undermine the value of this work for teachers. The importance of this work, nevertheless, remains upheld: Developing more intelligent habits of mind is linked to the development of better decision making in children.

Before leaping ahead to more recent developments in the area of moral development in children, a few words must be added about Leon Festinger's early work on *cognitive dissonance* (1957)—and his theory that cognitive dissonance exists and is a motivating state in human beings. Festinger's theory has so far not been identified with moral development, but it is cited here because within it lies an important awareness of how cognitive dissonance may be related to work in raising levels of moral awareness.

According to Festinger, cognitive dissonance gives rise to activity oriented toward reducing or eliminating the dissonance—that is, "successful reduction of dissonance is rewarding in the same sense that eating when one is hungry is rewarding." Festinger's research on his theory lends substantial support to the rationale of using dilemmas that create cognitive dissonance for students' belief systems, rocking and shaking them (cognitively) into reconsidering their positions and reevaluating beliefs in order to reduce the dissonance, because cognitive dissonance is not a happy state in which we can easily live our lives.

The more recent research of Paul Bloom (2010) at Yale University's Infant Cognition Center adds important information about the development of morality in even young children. In his studies, Bloom found that moral sense can be seen very early in life. He observed that as early as six months of age, even babies showed preferences for those who were "helpers" rather than those who were "hinderers." Bloom concluded from his studies that "people have a rudimentary sense of justice from a very early age." He also observed that "this doesn't make people naturally good. But it does mean that morality falls on prepared ground." As David Brooks (2010) wrote, "We come equipped to learn fairness and other virtues."

Steven Pinker (2008), writing in *The New York Times*, described what he calls the *moral sense*—a sense equated with the five others that rule human behavior:

> The human moral sense turns out to be an organ of considerable complexity, with quirks that reflect its evolutionary history and its neurobiological foundations.... Morality is not just any old topic in psychology but close to our conception of the meaning of life. Moral goodness is what gives each of us the sense that we are worthy human beings. We seek it in our friends and mates, nurture it in our children, advance

it in our politics and justify it with our religions. A disrespect for morality is blamed for everyday sins and history's worst atrocities.

Pinker advises that the science of the moral sense can be seen as a way to strengthen this fertile ground, by clarifying what morality is and how it should steer our actions. To that end, he suggests that "the starting point for appreciating that there *is* a distinctive part of our psychology for morality is seeing how moral judgments differ from other kinds of opinions we have on how people ought to behave."

The idea that the moral sense is an innate part of human nature is at the root of Pinker's theory; and that the "stirrings of morality emerge early in childhood" support the research of those like Bloom (2010), Turiel (2002), and Smetana and Killan (2013). Pinker's thesis that "the moral sense may be rooted in the design of the normal human brain" supplies further testimony for the evolutionary biologists. Yet, he admits that the idea is incomplete—that morality is something larger than our inherited moral sense:

> Moral truths may exist in some abstract Platonic realm, there for us to discover, perhaps in the same way that mathematical truths are there for us to discover. . . . Perhaps we are born with a rudimentary moral sense and as soon as we build on it with moral reasoning the nature of moral reality forces us to some conclusions but not to others. (Pinker, 2008)

Adding to this theoretical background is the more recent evidence of what has been described as *moral pain*—"profound moral distress, arising from the realization that one has committed acts with real and terrible consequences" (Marin, 1981). What is to be made of this theory, if not to examine such behavioral responses in light of a deep-seated, physiological sense of one's own humanity and what it means to behave morally?

One example of moral pain is the trauma that many soldiers experience in the aftermath of what they have done on the battlefield. These psychological wounds are considered to be a result of not physical but moral injuries, and their results—a falling apart physically, headaches, night chills, joint pain, waves of nausea, eruptions of skin welts, chronic digestive problems—come from what veterans describe as a consequence of what they have had to do to harm others, consistently, repeatedly, and with no pause for reflection (Press, 2018).

"The psychic and emotional impact of seeing the carnage they have wrought, on a regular basis, day after day, with stress more acute and pervasive that is equal to physical wounds" (Press, 2018) is now considered to be the consequence of behaving in ways that are antagonistic to one's own sense of morality and humanity.

What is one to make of all of the above? How does all of the research, development, and accumulated knowledge about moral development and reasoning help teachers and parents in their work to help children strengthen their sense of moral values, or in other words, the development of more honorable behavior? What can be distilled from the more recent findings are the following principles upon which the materials in this book are based:

- Some moral sense does exist in the early childhood years and is a part of our evolutionary make-up.
- There is an important link between a person's intelligence and moral reasoning.
- Giving children opportunities to examine and reflect on moral issues, in the presence of nonjudgmental questions that call for examination of their ideas, will enable them, after time, to make wiser, more informed decisions and lead to more honorable actions.
- This can be effectively done by teachers and parents when they understand the materials and strategies that can be used to produce these results.
- If social norms fall on prepared ground, the basis for developing thoughtful and socially responsible behavior already exists. When this prepared ground can be further cultivated, seeded, and sown, there is a very good chance that children will develop a higher moral sense. If this prepared ground is allowed to lie uncultivated, moral behavior is not only unlikely to blossom but is more likely to be laid waste.
- Admonishing children to accept authoritative answers in the absence of intelligent thought is a poor way to build moral development. Nor is "Do as I say, not as I do" a motivation for more moral behavior.

TWO

Making Sense of a Complex World

What's the Right Thing to Do?

A lawyer finds evidence that her potential client is guilty of a crime. Does the lawyer take the case? Does the lawyer do everything she can to defend the client, despite her knowledge that the client is guilty? What are the moral issues involved? What should the lawyer do?

A boy sees his friend taking some school supplies from the teacher's desk when no one else is looking. Does the boy tell on his friend? Does the boy observe the "rules of friendship" and not betray his friend? What should the boy do?

A teenage girl has been invited to an all-night party at the home of one of her friends, whose parents are away for the weekend. She knows that her own parents would not permit her to go—but she wants very much to go. Should she lie to her parents and tell them that she is going to a different friend's house to spend the night? Should she obey her parents, even though she thinks that her parents are being too strict with her? Should she argue with her parents and try to persuade them that she is responsible enough to go? What are the issues involved? What should she do? What are the potential consequences of those choices?

Her boyfriend wants her to pose for a nude selfie with her smartphone and send it to him. He has promised that he will not exploit the photo but keep it for himself. She thinks that if she doesn't comply, she might lose his friendship. Her girlfriends encourage her to take and send the photo. Her parents would be outraged. Does the friendship of this boy depend on her taking the photo and giving it to him? Can she trust his promise not to send the photo to his friends? What should she do?

The man is sitting on the street, with his back leaning against the shop window. His clothes are dirty, and his hair is disheveled. He has his overturned cap on the sidewalk, with the expectation of a hand-out. He has written a sign saying, "I'm an alcoholic. I need money to buy beer. Please help." Should passersby donate money to his cause? Is his honesty a motivator to help him or to shun him? Should he be ignored or helped? What's the right thing to do?

The teacher is marking the student's math paper. The student, who is trying very hard, has still not grasped the concepts of division of fractions and has made many errors in computation. What should the teacher write on the paper? How can he point out the errors while still encouraging the student to keep trying? What should the teacher do?

It is a truism to say that we live in a complex world, a world of rapid and increasing change, a world of ambiguity and uncertainty. In nearly every profession and walk of life, those who are making decisions confront many and confusing choices where there are no "right answers" and where choices are burdened with variables that involve not only principled action, but factors of expediency, cost-effectiveness, time limitations, humanity, and—not least—self-interest. But what does that mean for teachers and children?

It surely means that the options available to all of us are not only more varied but hold more uncertainties. And in the presence of these varied and uncertain choices, it is more difficult for adults to make decisions that are thoughtful, wise, and socially responsible. And if that is the case for adults, imagine how much more bewildering it is for young children to know the right thing to do, as they are faced with different points of view, a variety of options, and uncertain consequences.

But making choices is one of the more fundamental acts of life. Almost every action we take requires that choices be made. Knowing how to choose wisely, to choose after reflection, and to "own" our choices enable us to live healthier and more productive and satisfying lives. And while there is growing evidence that our values-related choices have biological origins, there is no doubt that the skills of making wise and informed and socially responsible decisions are cultivated with years of practice and reflection on practice—repeated opportunities to choose followed by critical analysis of how we came to that choice and what values we hold that have led us to that option. As David Brooks (2010) has written, "Social norms fall upon prepared ground. We come equipped to learn fairness and other virtues."

WHAT CAN TEACHERS AND PARENTS DO?

It is not surprising that the burden of "character development" is now being added to the school curriculum. In earlier times, it was primarily the home and religious teaching that played important roles in building moral development. And while these two building blocks of moral development still play important roles in many children's lives, it is within the organization of the school that children have the most frequent and extensive opportunities to reveal behavior that demands attention to their moral development.

This is not new, for it has been the teacher's job, historically, to deal with behavior. How this is done, and how effectively the treatments address character building, is at the heart of this book. These applications also serve for parents and caregivers, whose primary responsibilities are the health and welfare of their young charges.

Work in character education is not new. There are many professionals and organizations that address character development in school settings. For example, Mary Gordon's (2005) high-profile work throughout Canada and the United States teaches "roots of empathy" in workshops and in written materials to enable children to become more caring and more respectful of each other.

Thomas Lickona has been active in writing and conducting workshops to foster the integration of character development into every curriculum area: "When we think about the kind of character education we want for our children, it is clear that we want them to be able to judge what is right, care deeply about what is right, and then do what they believe to be right—even in the face of pressure from without and temptation from within" (Lickona, Schaps, & Lewis, 2006).

The Character Education Partnership (character.org) offers lectures, workshops, and written materials to provide teachers and school districts with the resources to promote character development.

This book goes beyond what is available in the literature and in the organizations that offer professional development in that it provides tools for teachers and parents to enable the link between children's thinking and moral development—tools that are at the heart of promoting thoughtful and socially responsible behavior in the early childhood years.

These materials and strategies are offered not only to teachers but to parents and all others who have a mind to continue to foster and develop the "better angels" of our nature in the care and education of young children.

THREE
Children as Decision Makers

At the library, Maya, age 3, picks out a book for herself and works her way over to the chairs and tables. Although there are many empty chairs, she sits down next to a small boy who, with a book in front of him, is staring ahead. Maya asks the boy if he would like her to read a story to him. Although she cannot read, she tells the story in her own words, using the images as clues and turning the pages appropriately. The boy is engrossed in the story and Maya smiles at him at the end. "Did you like the story?" she asks him. He nods his head. Maya leaves the table and walks over to her mother.

"Why did you choose to sit with that boy, Maya? There were so many empty chairs around."

"He looked sad and lonely. I wanted to read him a story to cheer him up."

Maya has never been "taught" in the instructional sense of the word to behave with a concern for others. Her parents, however, have taught her by example, and by allowing her choices and respecting those choices when her decisions did not involve danger to health or safety. They also make it a practice to explain the reasons for more humane and more caring choices to be made. These strategies have been used since she was old enough to understand—even before she was able to articulate choices in her own voice.

As she grows, in the presence of these strategies, she becomes more thoughtful, more respectful, more sensitive to the feelings of others. What biological endowments she has have been further developed by thoughtful, attentive, and intelligent parents. She is growing to become the kind of person that all teachers would love to have in their classes.

But not all parents have this understanding of child-rearing, nor do they have the time, the professional acumen, or the resources to follow a course of action that leads to honorable and caring behavior in their offspring. Not all children are blessed with Maya's parents. Alas.

In observing Maya's parents' strategies, it is easy to see that there are two important components of their "teaching." One is the many and varied opportunities Maya has to make her own choices—within, of course, the parameters of her health and safety. The second is the way her parents illuminate the rationale behind her choices, stressing the thinking behind them and articulating that thinking for her to reflect upon. Thinking and choosing—that is, choice, with reflection on choice—are the key ingredients of character building.

In another incident that tells a different story, an Asian American college student had pledged for the Pi Delta Psi fraternity at Baruch College. As part of his hazing, Mr. Deng was forced to run through a gauntlet of his fraternity brothers, across a frozen yard, blindfolded, with a backpack loaded with 30 pounds of sand. As Mr. Deng tried to negotiate his burden through the thuggish behavior of the group, he was repeatedly kicked, pushed, and punched, with force enough to cause severe brain and body injuries.

Although the frat boys recognized that Deng was badly injured and unconscious, and although they tried to revive him, they neglected to phone for an ambulance "because the cost was too high." After three more hours, they drove him to the hospital, where he died of his injuries (Rojas & Mueller, 2015).

Reading about such incidents gives pause to adults; we wonder how these young boys, who no doubt come from respectable families, could, as part of a group, unleash such violence on a fellow student whose only issue was to want to belong to that particular fraternity of Asian Americans. What has happened to the "selfish gene" that gives rise to their humanity, their caring, their honorable behavior, their empathy for a fellow human being? With no motivation to harm, no apparent reason other than the "fun" of the game, where do such urges come from in "normal, respectable boys"?

The pathologically disturbed interpersonal behavior leaves in question whether the basic groundwork of our development and being—empathy—has been, somehow, consistently and in large measure, numbed. The "rudimentary sense of justice" that people have from an early age (Bloom, 2010), while nascent in these boys, seems not to have been given any chance for growth, nurturing, and development. If morality falls on prepared ground, the ground on which morality fell for these young men was neither cultivated nor harvested.

THINKING AND DECIDING

Life is about making choices. From the moment of waking to the time we finish the day, we engage in actions that require choices to be made. Should I wear my skirt or my jeans? Should I wear my jacket or sweater? Should I have toast or cereal? Should I ride my bike or take the school bus? Should I take a lunch or buy one at school? What shall I tell my teacher about why I forgot to do my homework? My mother told me to leave my cell phone at home—but I really want to take it with me to school, and I can't decide whether to sneak it in my backpack. I'm supposed to go home right after school, but some of my friends are going over to the playground and I want to go with them. My mother wants me to practice the piano after school, but I'd rather play basketball with my friends.

Many of the decisions we face each day are inconsequential and offer no significant challenges. We make them easily, without giving them the mind space that more weighty decisions require.

Decisions with moral and ethical dimensions are not so easily dismissed, and it will come as no surprise that choosing the "right" thing to do is both difficult and sometimes even stressful. And in making those choices, the answers are, more often than not, ambiguous, uncertain, and subject to different points of view and different pressures. In other words, in many decisions of consequence, there are no "right" answers. And that is why such weighty matters are so nettlesome. It is, however, the moral scale upon which we weigh such issues that guides us in the choice.

The bottom line in promoting and developing moral behavior is for parents and teachers to "sow" that prepared moral ground so that young children may grow to become more like the Mayas and less like the frat boys. There are, alas, no quick fixes. But the data weigh heavily on the side of the strategies and interventions that adults might use to give children a chance to think about their choices, to see consequences of their actions, and to reflect on whether what they choose is "right and good"—in other words, on the side of developing a moral sense. As Derek Bok has written, "We need to teach children to think more carefully about ethical problems by making them discuss dilemmas that arise frequently in personal and professional life—because this enables them to become more thoughtful, more reasoned in their judgments" (Bok, 2008, p. 147).

SOME CAVEATS

Before launching into the chapters that spell out in detail those strategies and accompanying materials, it's important to make clear some caveats that are embedded in this work, for what is being proposed here may not be for every teacher or for every parent.

First, if children are to be allowed to think and choose for themselves, the data support the importance of interactive strategies that are nonjudgmental—that is, that allow children the freedom to choose for themselves (Stixrud & Johnson, 2018). Parents and teachers who are inclined to judgment, who believe that "telling children what is right and wrong" without allowing them the freedom of choice, may take issue with such a position.

Be that as it may, if children are to be allowed to find their own ways, make their own intelligent examinations of issues, and feel safe to explore and decide, the better way to do this is by allowing them a judgment-free exchange of ideas to make up their minds. The exception to this caveat has to do with issues of health and safety, when adult intervention is demanded.

When Louis Raths (Raths, Harmin, & Simon, 1973) proposed such an idea, he was condemned in the academy as someone who "didn't care if his sons grew up to become bank robbers." That was seen as the result of nonjudgmental exchanges. Nothing could be further from the truth. A nonjudgmental exchange in which children may make their own choices is not a vacuum. And when adult questioning that provides an impetus for thoughtful and analytical examination of the issues is part of the dialogue, the choice is grounded in thoughtful consideration and not tossed off without thought.

In addition, we adults are exemplars in that environment, and our behavior is a model for children; it reveals our own values, beliefs, and choices. We adults are not value-free, even as we ask children to consider, for themselves, what their choices are. "Moral freedom means that individuals should determine for themselves what it means to lead a good and virtuous life" (Bok, 2008, p. 169).

Second, the adult-child discussions that are described in later chapters require not only a nonjudgmental stance but also an absence of closure. Because so many of us are more comfortable with closure than we are with "ideas left hanging in the balance," this may be a tough call. But leaving issues that are being examined "in process"—rather than bringing them to resolution—is an essential ingredient in allowing children to continue to reflect, even when the discussions have been concluded. The raising of questions that create cognitive dissonance (Festinger, 1957) brings about the kind of mental processing from which children's beliefs and choices become clearer as they continue to process, even after the questioning has ceased.

A third caveat concerns adults' own disclosures of their values and beliefs. For even when teachers and parents engage children using nonjudgmental responses and questions in the examination of moral issues, there *are* times when adults reveal their own values, outside of and apart from the values-oriented discussions. Adults should not feel obliged never to tell what they think about what is right and what is the right thing for *them* to do. These disclosures can and should take place outside of the interpersonal dialogue in which children are free to make up their own minds. If adults are exemplars of morality, children can learn a great deal from them about what is important to them, about what they prize and care for, about what they think is right.

When children reveal values that are at odds with adults' stated views, it's more difficult for those adults to remain nonjudgmental. But no one said it was easy.

A fourth caveat concerns issues that are best left untouched in the school discussions about what the "right thing to do" is. These include religious beliefs and cultural mores that come from homes where certain ways of thinking and behaving may or may not be counter to the school ethos. The position taken here is that parents' rights about religious and cultural values need to be respected and not undermined.

FREEDOM TO CHOOSE AND EMPOWERMENT

As morality seems to have a biological basis, it also may be observed that one's sense of personal power—that is, the "power to"—is also a part of one's emotional needs (Wassermann, 1990). Like our basic needs for love, belonging, and emotional security, we seem also have the need for "power to" inherent in our human makeup.

William Glasser (1985), in his book *Control Theory in the Classroom*, tells us that "all of our behavior is always our best attempt to satisfy at least five powerful forces which, because they are built into our genetic structure, are best called basic needs." One is the physiological need to stay alive and reproduce; the other four, all psychological needs, are "belonging (which includes love), power, freedom and fun." Everything we do may thus be seen as aimed at satisfying one or more of these needs.

If the development of a sense of "power to" is accepted as yet one more emotional need that forms a part of our set of basic human needs, it also follows that it must be adequately satisfied in the early childhood years if children are to grow into adults who believe in their own capability—that is, "can-do" adults. Power-to needs are fed when adults allow children choices, so that even very young children may exercise their own options in situations that genuinely matter to them. Giving children choices implicitly communicates that we believe in them and in their ability.

When the option to choose for oneself is taken away by others who exercise the options in their behalf, children become frustrated, even enraged. Through such adult actions, children learn that they are not to be trusted to decide for themselves. They learn not that they can do but that they can't do. They learn to doubt themselves. When their drives for power-to continue to be thwarted, children are likely to show increased frustration and anger that reveal themselves in acts of aggression. It is no wonder that adults with frustrated power-to needs desire power-over, a compensatory behavior that never fulfills the innate power-to need (Wassermann, 1990).

When children are given choices, when they are allowed to decide for themselves, when their choices are respected, they grow to believe in themselves. They begin to see themselves as "can-do" people. They grow to believe that they have some control over their lives. It is not clear why this is so, but exercising one's power-to is enormously satisfying (Wassermann, 1990).

A child whose needs for personal power have been adequately met is much more open to develop a moral sense. Children with unmet power-to needs, who need to sublimate them in the need to exert power over others, are much less likely candidates for moral development. Trying to teach a bully, for example, to respect the feelings of others may be as remote as hoping to win the lottery.

Like growing flowers, where certain specific conditions are provided to produce beautiful blossoms, adults supply the conditions that establish the growing ground for empowered, moral children. These conditions include, of course, provision for children's physical safety and well-being as well as emotional nurturance, respect for children as persons, and respect for their right to exercise their own choices. These are some of the building blocks of empowerment—and morality.

FOUR
Introduction to the World of Moral Dilemmas

In the chapters that follow, a variety of materials as well as discussion strategies are presented that engage young children in the examination of moral dilemmas. The materials include mini-cases—anecdotes that come from the lives of young children, about which they are asked to reflect on what they believe is "right" and what they consider to be "wrong." Also included are suggestions for children's books and films that center on moral issues. A subsequent chapter is devoted to the kinds of discussion skills that parents and teachers may use to further children's thinking about "the right thing to do."

The value of small-group work in classrooms is also highlighted, and suggestions are made about how to orient the children so that small groups can become more effective in their interpersonal interactions and exploration of issues.

IT'S COMPLICATED

History, literature, films, and real life are rich with examples of moral dilemmas that people face as they wrestle with the question, What's the right thing to do? Arguably one of the most well known among these is Hamlet's "To be, or not to be," as he famously states, "That is the question." But one doesn't have to fall back on Shakespeare to find an abundance of incidents in which children and adults search for the best way, the right way, the choice that is close to what we hold dear. There are numerous examples in history as well as in current events that add to our understanding of what it means to make moral choices.

Sometimes the dilemmas people face are profound and have life and death consequences. Anne Frank and her family were hidden in the attic of a Dutch family's house to keep them safe from the Nazi occupiers of the Netherlands during World War II. When the Dutch family was betrayed, its members as well as all those who were hidden in the attic were taken as prisoners and murdered. The Dutch family made a conscious choice and put their lives at risk to help those in danger. They believed that it was morally "right" to do so.

Sir Thomas More wrestled with his conscience when King Henry VIII asked him to sanction the king's divorce of his first wife, Catherine of Aragon, so that he might be free to marry Ann Boleyn. In defiance of the king, More, a devout Catholic, refused. He was executed, but he had remained faithful to his belief in the sanctity of marriage.

President Harry Truman struggled over his decision to give his assent to the dropping of the first atomic bomb on the city of Hiroshima. The issues that he considered in his decision were, on one side, the potential earlier end to the war between Japan and the United States, and on the other, the annihilation of an entire city of civilians as a warning to the Japanese of the power of this new weapon.

Ruth Macklin's *Mortal Choices* (1987) offers more than a dozen case histories that present real-life ethical dilemmas in modern medicine—situations that adults who have faced medical issues themselves will find familiar territory. Alan Lockwood and David Harris (1985) describe a selected group of ethical problems in the history of the United States—for example, the Salem Witch trials, the conflicts between Native Americans and the white settlers, and the support of slavery in the southern states, to name a few—demonstrating that those with decision-making powers in government frequently faced ethical dilemmas with resolutions that depended on where their values lay and that their choices led to consequences that are felt centuries later.

Sometimes moral decisions are less perilous, but nevertheless still nettlesome.

A family chooses to open their home to new immigrants to help them get settled in their new land, Canada. They have made a conscious choice to help others in need at some cost and inconvenience to themselves. Their neighbors take issue with them for housing people of color in the neighborhood.

A school chum who has not had time to do an assignment asks you to let him copy your paper, to submit it as his own to his teacher. He is a good friend to you, but what he is asking seems like cheating.

A woman is cutting flowers from a bush in the city park for her own use. There is a law that prohibits people from harming the foliage of the park. You see her doing this. She is an older lady, and maybe she is not aware of the law. Maybe she doesn't care. Do you just walk away and ignore her? Do you tell her what she is doing is wrong? Do you find someone to report her to?

You see some bullies mocking a homeless person. The homeless person appears to be drunk. Do you play a role here in defending the homeless man? Do you confront the bullies and shame them for their behavior? Do you walk away, thinking, "It's none of my business"?

Life and death moral dilemmas are usually made with considerable thought about the choices and the consequences of the action. Other values-laden choices, while neither perilous nor of major consequence to self, are less onerous but nevertheless demanding. In either group, there are no "right" answers to the dilemmas; there is only the individual's position on what is right and good for him or her. In making our choices, our action reveals what values we hold dear, what's important to us, what we prize above all else. "People are what they do, not what they say," writes James Lee Burke (2018). How we behave, not what we claim to care about, reveals to the world who we are and what we stand for.

The position taken here is that when a child is of several minds about his or her choice, it is a given that self-awareness—that is, the consciousness of how that choice is being made—is an important contributor to growing morality. To choose rashly, without considered thought in matters of consequence, is to act impulsively, perhaps irrationally, and often with unintended consequences. In retrospect, we may think, Why on earth did I ever do that?—often too little, too late.

To think, to make a conscious choice before acting, is a mark of moral awareness. That is why, in engaging children in the examination of their decisions about moral issues, the adult's questions to the child that invite his or her critical reflection about the nature of the choice are a key factor in illuminating the thinking behind the decision. Choosing without reflection, without critical examination of how one arrived at that decision, does little to add to insightfulness and self-awareness.

It is important to remember, as well, that moral judgments differ from other kinds of decisions. Choosing whether to put on a red or blue tie, whether to have tuna fish or salmon for lunch, whether to ride a bike or walk to school are not in the same ballpark as whether to make a conscious effort to take the old paint cans across town to the recycling center or whether to just dump them into the garbage.

Making a choice in matters of consequence to self is often not easy. Sometimes expedience overrules "the right thing to do." In addition, what's "right" for Henry may not be "right" for Henrietta. We may believe strongly in the need to recycle, but going across town to deliver the old paint cans may be a trip too far. Yet, if our moral sense is strong enough and if we choose expediency over morality, we may find ourselves feeling guilty and perhaps even ashamed. And when our choice offends deeply held values about life and limb, the result may be "moral pain" (Press, 2018)—the inability to live with oneself in the aftermath of that abrogation of what one deeply believes.

What confounds choices as well are incidents where the issues are not clear, when the data are conflicting, when not all the data are available, when it's hard to make sense of what's right. Sometimes, one has to choose something that is not totally satisfying, because that is the best alternative among several less than good choices. Sometimes, it's just too difficult to consider the best choice among alternatives; it's easier to just plunge in and act.

Making a choice that protects something that one values, something that leads to consequences that are clearly seen, is the path that demands reflection on who one is and what one stands for. In that process, we grow to understand ourselves better; we grow to know ourselves as persons with moral integrity. There is, of course, a strong relationship between making a moral choice that is a tough decision, on the one hand, and one's sense of empowerment, on the other. We feel good about what we have done and that feeds our ego strength.

Alas, there is no direct path to right and wrong; the best we can hope for is a better awareness of the kind of thinking that lies behind our choices: a clarity of who we are, what we believe in, and what the implications of our choices are.

Critical incidents from stories, history, films, current events, and the lived experiences of the children will offer a large depository of materials in which children may be asked, "What's the right thing to do?" A list of children's books and films that present moral issues are offered in the next chapter. A selection of mini-cases are included that provide examples of what constitutes narratives with moral dilemmas. These can be chosen for discussion, and they should be chosen in relationship to their relevance to the children's own experiences.

The caveat is that whatever is chosen for discussion, narratives or anecdotes or incidents that are too sensitive, in a teacher's or parent's judgment, are best avoided. Putting children in situations where they may feel harassed or "put on the spot" or in any way stressed is far from the objective of these exercises. A teacher's or parent's sensitive judgment, knowledge of the children, and understanding of what is important in their lives make up a good rule of thumb to guide the adult's choices.

To go a step further, it should be mentioned that in examining these exercises that present moral dilemmas, it is less important that children choose what they consider right but more important that they examine the process that leads them to those decisions. In short, the *examination*—raising levels of cognitive awareness of how the decisions are being made—is where the larger payoffs lie.

ADULT-CHILD DISCUSSIONS ABOUT MORAL ISSUES

Putting children into situations where they are asked to reflect on a story, narrative, or lived experience that calls for making judgments is only one side of the coin in promoting their thoughtful reflection about their choices. The other side is the use of the teacher's or parent's responses to children's statements. The stories, anecdotes, or incidents are not, in and of themselves, enough. Children's responses to them need to be examined, with key ideas and key issues brought out that lead to the illumination of various points of view and to their choices.

Responses and questions also serve to highlight problems that may have no definitive or "good" answers. Such interactions disabuse children of seeking "right" answers when there are no right answers. This, too, is an important dimension of these discussions. Before embarking on the chapter that describes these discussion strategies in detail, several points need mentioning.

The first, and most obvious, is that children's ideas and statements need to be heard. That is, the adult puts aside other matters, makes eye contact with the child, and listens carefully and respectfully to what is being said—without interrupting. In both verbal and nonverbal actions, the adult demonstrates, with spoken words and attentive behavior, that the child is being heard. The importance of this strategy—both verbal and nonverbal—cannot be overestimated. It communicates: "I hear you. I am listening to what you have to say. Your ideas are important to me."

This is easier said than done, for when adults have a variety of other issues pulling at them and demanding their attention, to give a child the full attention that his or her statement warrants means putting all other distractions aside and making a concerted effort to show respectful attention to the child's ideas. Unless this first step can be demonstrated, the rest is folly.

Second, the adult—the parent or teacher—responds by reflecting back the child's statement, and this is done without bias, without any facial indication that what the child has said is not acceptable. The result of this reflective response is to indicate that the child's idea has been nonjudgmentally heard. It is "played back" so that the child may hear it again and may consider it further. In other words, the child's spoken statement does not drift off into the ether. It is "working material" for further consideration.

This playing back is better done in a paraphrase than in a simple repetition of the statement. That gives the child a new way of looking at what he or she has said so that it may be affirmed, denied, or reconsidered. Here again, the emphasis is on giving the child an opportunity to examine and reexamine his or her thinking, setting in motion the cognitive processing that is at the heart of more thoughtful consideration of one's beliefs.

Third, as the interactive dialogue ensues, the adult uses the kinds of questions that prod the child to think further about what he or she has said—about the importance of it, about the possible consequences, about why he or she thinks it is "good." The types of questions that can be used in such situations are presented in the chapter on discussion strategies, and the list of them is perhaps like showing a budding pianist a list of notes that make up Grieg's *Piano Concerto*.

It takes some practice and a great deal of reflection on practice to master these discussion skills. But the good news is that even when errors in using inappropriate questions or responses are made, the sky doesn't fall. One can play a few wrong notes and still be able to hear the music.

The interactions that call for a child's further thinking about his or her belief statements cannot work successfully unless they are done in a nonjudgmental way and with a great deal of respect shown for the child and his or her thoughts. This is easier when the child's beliefs are in accord with what the teacher or parent believes, but it's much harder when the child takes a position that is contrary to the adult's. Once again, practice, and reflection on practice while engaging in the discussion, is the important element in becoming proficient.

When the interactive dialogue works successfully, the end result is to leave the child in a state of ambiguity. Nothing is resolved, and that is another essential ingredient to his or her further thinking, reflecting, and contemplating on what was said, what was meant, what was important, and what was "good." It is for the child to think, reflect, and finally resolve the issue for him or herself, making the choice and deciding, based on what is important, about what he or she holds dear.

There will be times, of course, when an adult—teacher or parent—cannot in good conscience accept nonjudgmentally what a child has said. In such cases—and these are best left to the discretion of the adult in charge—it is an adult's obligation to state his or her own values. When this is done respectfully, it allows the adult to own his or her own moral ground and sets the example that an adult has values that are different from what the child believes. The way this is effectively done lies in the way the adult uses the discussion strategies described in a later chapter, never condemning, never belittling, never ridiculing. An example is:

> I know you believe it's okay for you to make fun of a person's clothing if it looks odd to you. But I want you to know, Dennis, that I don't share that belief because I worry that if you do that, it will very likely hurt that person's feelings. But I'm happy to hear if you have something more you want to say about it.

When parents and teachers can use such methods to enable children to become more thoughtful decision makers, to choose more wisely, to answer for themselves, "What's the right thing to do?" they have given them perhaps one of the greatest gifts of child development — respect and the chance to lead more purposeful and more socially responsible lives.

THE VALUE OF SMALL-GROUP WORK

A teacher of many years' experience once remarked that small-group work had no intrinsic value, since when students got together in groups, they were "merely exchanging ignorances." This is hardly borne out by the data. Children as young as five and six can benefit from an interchange of ideas that occurs in small working groups (Wassermann, 1989; Wassermann & Ivany, 1996; Wasik, 2008).

Of course, the precondition is that learning to work effectively in groups does not come by fiat. Successful group work is a learned skill, and for teachers who want to pursue small-group work as an a priori step to whole class discussion, it is probably a very good idea to provide the parameters and the guidelines for group work, take some time to watch and listen, and provide feedback, so that when push comes to shove, and important discussions are at stake, the children are already primed and ready to tackle more serious issues.

One of the many benefits of small-group work is that the children have a chance to put out their ideas to each other in a safe and controlled environment. Other, implicit benefits include the building of spoken language skills, learning to listen to other's ideas, and learning to take turns and wait one's turn respectfully. The sense of empowerment that children feel when they have control of the environment in the small group cannot be overestimated.

Teaching children about working successfully in small groups is a matter of orienting them to the process. One way to do this is to begin by asking children for their ideas about how they might best work in small groups, and creating a chart of "good group habits" that gets posted on the wall for all to see and refer to as needed. The likelihood is great that even young children will come up with ideas that are both useful, respectful, and workable. Alternatively, teachers may create their own list of "good group discussion behaviors" and post these for children to use as reference.

There is, also, much benefit to a whole-class discussion, post hoc, about how well the small groups worked that day, what went wrong, what might be done next time to improve them. In that way children learn more about effective group functioning and how to make the best use of their small-group time.

In concluding this chapter, it's important to remind ourselves, as Brooks (2010) has written, that "social norms fall on prepared ground." Many young children who will be participants in work that asks them to examine "what's the right thing to do" may already have a well-developed sense of "right and wrong," and the work that teachers and parents do with them will fall on "prepared ground." There is likely to be a small few whose sense of justice and morality, like a flowering plant that has languished for lack of water, has already been allowed to wither and dry up.

    The former group will be a joy to teach—more open, more accessible, more aware; the latter group, more challenging. Different children begin at different points on the "morality scale." For the adults who work with these differences, the task is the same, but progress and measures of success are likely to proceed at different rates. However, even for the more challenging children, there is hope. As a sixth grader reminded his teacher, "Good teachers must have love, even for the bad ones."

FIVE

Stories, Mini-Cases, Books, Films, and Classroom Incidents

This long chapter is divided into four parts, each offering selected examples from literature, animated films, classroom incidents, and mini-cases that are related to the experiences of young children. This chapter and the two that follow are the meat and potatoes of how parents and teachers can engage young children in discussions and query them about their thoughts on what's the right thing to do. The incidents and mini-cases are prototypes—in other words, only examples. They can be lifted from the pages and used either per se or as models for teachers and parents to create alternative versions that better reflect the experiences of the children.

Some examples are more "sensitive"—tapping into topics that may be more stressful for some children. Some are less so. Choosing, then, should be done with an eye and ear to what is more appropriate for a particular group or for a particular child. Once again, topics that create anxiety or unhappiness or discomfort for children should be avoided. It is not the intention of any of these materials to put children in situations that are emotionally stressful for them. When working with groups, teachers may certainly use their discretion in excusing any child from participating if such an action is warranted by the adult's observation of the child's discomfort in the situation.

Each story, film, classroom incident, or mini-case is captioned with a "big idea"—that is, the main theme, a central discussion point about morality and behavior. Each is also followed by two or three questions that begin a discussion that should lead to the main issue: What's the right thing to do? The questions begin with a request to summarize the story or event as well as a request to examine the data about the characters. Working from this basis of data gathering gives children experience in using data to inform their choices, habituating them to the importance of examining data as an a priori condition in making decisions of consequence.

Chapter 6 adds other ideas for experiences that can engage children in putting moral behavior into action. It includes suggestions for work on community projects and one-on-one tutoring.

The kinds of discussion skills that tap into children's thinking about moral issues are found in chapter 7.

MINI-CASES

Teaching with cases has a long and successful history as a pedagogy that was pioneered at the Harvard Business School in the mid-20th century and has become "one of the highlights of the HBS experience." It has been championed by professors as well as by high school and elementary school teachers who have been witness to the observable and tangible effects of the pedagogy on positive learning outcomes. The claims that students learn to communicate their ideas more effectively, are able to examine complicated issues in more critical ways, and improve their ability to make good decisions have been documented in numbers of articles and books (Christensen, Garvin, & Sweet, 1991; Adam, 1992; Ewing, 1990; Wassermann, 1994).

Students are among those who are also enthusiasts about their involvement with cases:

> If you can believe what the students tell you, they say that they continue to think about the issues long after the course is over. They say that the habits of thinking built during the class discussions endure and are used to their advantage in other classes. Some say they still discuss the issues talked about in class, even now. I think if students are still thinking about issues in your course 3 to 5 years later, and are able to use habits of thinking to their advantage in other courses, well, that can't be too bad a job of teaching, eh? (Wassermann, 1994, p. 17)

Cases put students in the role of decision makers where there are no simple solutions to the dilemmas, no "right answers." Yet, "through the dynamic process of exchanging perspectives, countering and defending points of view, and building on each other's ideas, students become adept at analyzing issues, exercising judgment and making difficult decisions" ("The HBS Case Method," n.d.).

Of course, this is not true for all students; but no strategy, if truth be told, works successfully for every student every time. To expect such success is to expect too much. If the vast majority benefits, is that enough?

WHAT'S A CASE?

The cases found in the contexts mentioned above are instructional tools, complex educational instruments that appear in the form of narratives. These cases usually include information and hard data, and while centered in specific subject areas, they are, by nature, interdisciplinary. Good cases highlight problems or "big ideas"—those significant issues in a subject that warrant serious, in-depth examination. The narratives are usually drawn from real-life problems confronting real people (Wassermann, 1994).

The mini-cases and classroom incidents included in this chapter are more elementary forms of the kinds of cases found in any collection of cases in case clearinghouses and textbooks. They have been written with an eye to the cognitive abilities and experiences of young children, especially for the "early childhood" years. Most of them are centered on issues that would be found close to young children's experiences with each other in class, in the school yard, and at home.

Cases about current social issues (e.g., racism, sexism, politics, immigration, security, economic opportunity, guns in school, etc.) have not been included, but teachers who go on to write their own mini-cases can tap into social issues when and if they are appropriate to children's developmental levels and experiences.

Teachers and parents who use the cases in this chapter have permission to take them from this text and duplicate them, if warranted, for individual or group use. Alternatively, for children who are not yet reading on their own, they may be read aloud, as one would read a storybook from the library. The mini-case is then followed up by asking the few questions that immediately follow each case, and these should begin a more extended discussion about "the right thing to do."

Children should be encouraged to respond, to tell what they think, to give their own ideas, and to express their views freely, without the adult passing judgment. This absence of judgment—either explicitly or in facial expression or tone of voice—is imperative in the free exchange of ideas that come from children. Children will not say truthfully what they think if they believe their ideas will be judged or if they believe they are not going to give the teacher or the parent the "right answer."

Once again, these mini-cases are prototypes, and teachers and/or parents should feel free to adapt them to make them more relevant to the lives of particular children.

Chapter 7, on discussion skills, provides many examples of how the discussion leader orchestrates an extended adult-student discussion about the issues in the cases.

Chapter 5

TWENTY-TWO MINI-CASES

1. Big idea: Is taking something that is prohibited okay if you are going to return it?

Arthur had his hands on the book he wanted to borrow on his library card. The book was called, *The Polar Bear Son: An Inuit Tale*. Arthur thought this would be a good story for his mother to read to him. He liked polar bears, but he also liked stories about all kinds of animals. When he went to the librarian's desk to check out the book, the librarian told him that that book did not circulate. That meant that you could only read it in the library. You were not permitted to take it home.

Arthur didn't understand that rule. Why couldn't you take the book home? Why did it have to be read only in the library? He didn't think that was fair. So what would happen if he slipped the book into his backpack, took it home, had his mother read it to him, and then returned it to the library the next day? No one would know. It wouldn't be stealing, would it?

   a. Tell the story in your own words.
   b. What was Arthur's dilemma?
   c. What should Arthur do? If you were his friend, what would you tell him? What makes you think that is a good idea?

2. Big idea: What's more important: going to school or taking some days off to go to work with Dad on his truck?

Millie's mom and dad were separated. She spent one week with her dad and the next week with her mother. When she was with her mother, her mother made sure she went to school every day. It was important, her mom said, not to miss a day of school unless you were sick.

When Millie was with her dad, he would ask her if she wanted to come with him on his job, driving a truck. He liked to take her along with him. It kept him company on his long trips. He didn't think it was so important for her to go to school every day.

Millie wanted to go with her dad. But she also knew that it was important for her not to miss a day of school if she was not sick. Her dad was standing at the door, asking her, "Millie, are you coming with me or not?"

   a. Tell the story in your own words.
   b. What was Millie's dilemma?
   c. What should Millie do? If you were her friend, what would you tell her? What makes you think that is a good idea?

3. Big idea: How do you manage to keep from punching your younger brother when he is such a pest?

Lalit is seven years old. His younger brother, Patel, is five. His parents always tell Lalit that he must be a good older brother and look after his younger brother and take care of him. That is the job of an older brother.

But Lalit thinks his brother is a pest. Patel sneaks into Lalit's room and takes his toys and hides them. He seems to think it's fun to play a trick on his older brother. When Lalit tells his parents about Patel, they tell him that Patel is younger and smaller and needs to be reminded not to do that.

But this time Patel has gone too far. He has taken Lalit's favorite Tyler the Tiger toy, and Lalit is furious. He wants to take revenge on Patel. He could go into Patel's room and break one of his toys. He could get back at Patel by punching him in the nose. What should Lalit do?

   a. Tell the story about Patel and Lalit in your own words.
   b. What does Patel do that makes Lalit so angry?
   c. Why do you suppose Patel does that? What ideas do you have about that?
   d. If you were Lalit's friend, what would you tell him to do? What makes you think that is a good idea?

4. Big idea: Is it better to confess the truth, at the risk of punishment, or to lie and pretend you are innocent?

Arlo was kicking a soccer ball around the house. His mother had told him many times that kicking a ball in the house was a no-no—that he could break something. The place for kicking a ball was out of doors—on the lawn or in the playground or on the field.

But it was raining, and Arlo was stuck inside. He had nothing to do. His mom said, "No TV until after dinner. And no tablet. You had your two hours of tablet time already today."

Arlo was stuck. He was sick and tired of his old toys. So when his mom was doing the laundry, he kicked that soccer ball and—*wham!*—it hit the lamp, and the lamp toppled over and fell to the floor and broke.

Mom heard the noise. "What was that, Arlo? What fell?" She came out of the laundry room and saw the broken lamp. "What happened Arlo? How did that lamp break?"

Arlo could tell her that a big wind blew through the open window and broke the lamp. Or he could tell her the truth. If he lied, he might avoid being punished. But if he told the truth, he would have to pay the consequences.

   a. Tell the story about Arlo in your own words.

b. What do you think Arlo did that was wrong? What ideas do you have about that?
c. If you were Arlo's friend, what would you tell him to do? What makes you think that's a good idea?
d. If you do something wrong, is it okay for you to have consequences? What do you think about that?

5. *Big idea: Is it okay to take something that is forbidden when no one knows about it?*

Penny's mom was baking chocolate chip cookies to take to school for a parent-teacher meeting. The smell of the chocolate chip cookies baking in the oven was making Penny's mouth water. Chocolate chip cookies were her favorites. But Mom said Penny was not to have any cookies from this batch. She needed all of them for the meeting. And besides, Penny should not be eating cookies before dinner. She would spoil her dinner.

The cookies came out of the oven—and there were a zillion of them. Surely not all of them were needed for the meeting. There were plenty of cookies to go around for all of the parents and teachers. If Penny sneaked up and took one or two, no one would notice. She didn't think one cookie would spoil her dinner.

Her mom went into the bedroom to get her coat, and Penny was left alone in the kitchen. She could hardly stand by and just watch those cookies go out the door. She was studying the cookies, trying to decide what she should do.

a. Tell the story about Penny in your own words.
b. Why would it be wrong to take a cookie if there were enough for the parent-teacher meeting and no one would notice?
c. What should Penny do? If you were her friend, what would you tell her? Why do you think that's a good idea?

6. *Big idea: Is it more important to tell the truth or to protect someone's feelings by being kind and untruthful?*

The first graders were out on the field, and they were choosing classmates for the two teams that would be playing soccer. The teacher chose Celeste to be the team leader of the Bears team. She could choose any of her classmates to be on her team. Bryce was chosen to be the team leader of the Wolves team. He could choose any of his classmates to be on his team.

The two teams would be competing against each other to see which team was best. It was important for the team leaders to choose the best players first—to make sure their own teams were the strongest and the most likely to win.

Celeste was making her choices fast. She knew who she wanted, and she began by picking the strongest players. Bryce looked over at his classmates and wondered. His best friend, Ibrahim, was a weak player. He knew that. But he also knew that Ibrahim was his friend, and he didn't want to hurt his feelings. So what should Bryce do? It would be kind to pick Ibrahim for his team. But it might hurt the team's chances of winning.

  a. Tell the story about Celeste and Bryce in your own words.
  b. What is Bryce's dilemma? Tell that in your own words.
  c. What, in your opinion, is more important: Being kind to Ibrahim and taking the chance of losing the game or passing Ibrahim up and choosing a stronger player?
  d. If you were Bryce's friend, what would you tell him to do? Why do you think that's a good idea?

7. *Big idea: Should you give away some of your food to someone who is hungry when you don't have enough for yourself?*

Sheila had a dollar to buy some food for her lunch. Her mother told her to be careful about the dollar, since, as Sheila knew, there was never enough money in their house. Sheila thought that a dollar was a lot of money and she used it to buy a slice of pizza and a carton of chocolate milk at the school cafeteria.

She picked a seat next to Brigitte, who had no food in front of her.

"Where's your lunch?" asked Sheila.

Brigitte put her head down, and her cheeks turned red. She was embarrassed.

And then Sheila knew. Brigitte had no lunch. And she didn't have any money to buy lunch for herself.

Sheila looked down at her small piece of pizza and her very small carton of chocolate milk. There was hardly enough to fill her own tummy; one dollar didn't buy a lot of food. But could she sit there and eat when she knew that Brigitte was as hungry as she was? Should she share the little she had or eat it all herself?

  a. Tell the story about Sheila and Brigitte in your own words.
  b. What can you say about Sheila and her dollar?
  c. What can you say about Brigitte?
  d. What should Sheila do? Why do you think that's a good idea?

8. *Big idea: How do you handle a situation when you are unjustly accused?*

The teacher was very angry! Someone had thrown a ball through the window of the principal's office and had broken the glass. No one was hurt, but the principal told the teachers to find out who did that. There would be consequences to pay.

The teacher knew that her class was in the school yard during recess and that they were playing with a ball and kicking it around.

"You have to tell me, boys and girls, who kicked that ball through the glass window. You have to be honest and tell me the truth. Who is responsible?"

The children were quiet. Only one boy knew who did it—and he was to blame. So instead of owning up to what he had done, he tried to put the blame on someone else.

Letitia raised her hand. "Yes, Letitia, what can you tell me?" asked the teacher.

"I saw who did it, Miss Boyer. It was Simpson. I saw him kick the ball."

Mrs. Boyer looked at Simpson with a very angry face. "Did you do that, Simpson?" she asked. "Tell the truth now. I want you to tell me the truth."

Simpson looked astonished. He hadn't kicked the ball. But he didn't know who had done it. So why was Letitia blaming him?

"I never did that, Miss Boyer. I don't know who did it, but it wasn't me."

"Well, Letitia would not make up a story if it wasn't true. So I'm going to have to punish you for doing that, Simpson. Your consequence will be no recess for you for two weeks. You'll have to sit in the classroom while the other children are outside playing, and I will have to report this to your parents."

Simpson put his head down on his desk. Why was he being blamed for something he hadn't done? Who was going to believe him now?

   a. Tell the story about Simpson in your own words.
   b. What does the story tell you about Letitia? What do you know about her?
   c. What does the story tell you about Simpson? What do you know about him?
   d. What should Simpson do now? If you were his friend, what would you suggest? Why would that be a good thing to do?

9. *Big idea: Is it okay to tell a secret when it means betraying a trust?*

Theo was afraid. He called his friend Colin, who he knew he could trust. They had been best friends since they were very small children. Their moms went to the same market, went to the PTA meetings together, and took turns driving Theo and Colin to school and to the playground. But Theo was in trouble, and he knew he could count on his friend Colin to help him out.

Colin picked up the phone and asked Theo, "What's up?" Colin felt that something must be wrong for Colin to be calling at that early hour in the morning. There was a long silence on the phone and Colin asked his friend again, "Hey Theo. What's happening?"

Theo began to talk—but his sentences weren't coming out right. Finally, Theo said, "I have to tell you something. But you have to promise never to tell a soul." Again, there was a long silence on the phone. Colin was quiet and waited for his friend to continue.

After a long wait, Theo said, "Mr. Smith offered to give me a ride home from school. I promised my mother I would never take a ride from anyone I didn't know, but I know Mr. Smith, don't I?"

Colin didn't answer but continued to wait. And Theo began to tell his secret.

"I didn't know what to do. He put his hand on my leg. I was scared. I told him I needed to get out of the car and I would walk home. He stopped the car and let me out. But he told me that we now had a secret and I wasn't to tell anyone."

Colin didn't know what to say. But then he said, "You should tell your mother or father. You really need to tell them."

Theo said, "I can't tell. I said I wouldn't tell. And if I did tell them, they'd punish me for getting into the car with Mr. Smith. So this has to be a secret. But I had to tell you. I had to tell someone. I was scared."

Colin wanted to keep his friend's secret. But he also thought he should tell an adult what had happened. Should he tell? Or should he keep Theo's secret?

   a. Tell this story about Colin and Theo in your own words.
   b. What is Theo's dilemma?
   c. Why do you suppose Theo is scared to tell his parents? What are your ideas about that?
   d. What should Colin do? Should he keep Theo's secret? Or should he tell his mom or dad what happened?

10. Big idea: Is it okay to tell a lie to get something you truly, deeply want if the lie doesn't hurt anybody?

The class was putting on a play about the Pilgrims' first Thanksgiving. Debbie was excited. Her class had never done a play before—and this play was going to be performed in the big auditorium for all the other classes to come and see. She thought she would die if she didn't get a part. She wanted a part so badly, she could hardly breathe.

Mrs. Franklin was asking about the parts now.

"Who wants to play the part of the mother?" Many children put up their hands, waving them in the air, trying to get Mrs. Franklin's attention. They all wanted to be chosen.

Finally, Mrs. Franklin picked Linda and asked her, "Linda, would you be able to get a costume to make you look like an older lady? A mom?"

Linda nodded her head up and down so fast, it might have fallen off her neck.

"Okay, Linda. The part is yours."

And that was that. There was only one more part and that was for the announcer.

Debbie was frantic. It was the very last part—her very last chance.

So when the teacher asked, "Who would like to have the part of the announcer?"

Debbie's hand went up so fast and so tall that it nearly reached the ceiling!

"Okay, Debbie. I see you really want that part. But you will need to wear a long black skirt and a white shirt—because the announcer has to look very proper. So do you have a long skirt and a white shirt to wear?"

Debbie looked down at her well-worn clothes. Her mom never had enough money to buy her new clothes, and her clothes mostly came from the thrift shops. Sometimes they were too big for her, and she felt ashamed to wear them. But she knew that her mother was doing the best she could do.

Debbie gulped down twice and looked Mrs. Franklin in the eye. "Yes," she said. "I have a long skirt and a white blouse, Mrs. Franklin."

Now Debbie had the part of the announcer. But what would she tell her mother?

a. Tell the story about Debbie and the play in your own words.
b. What can you tell us about Debbie? What kind of girl is she? What do you think?
c. Why do you suppose getting a part in the play is so important to Debbie? What do you think?
d. Is it okay for Debbie to have told a lie to her teacher in order to get the part she so badly wanted? What do you think about that?

11. *Big idea: What do I have to do to get some friends?*

Lucca had just moved into the neighborhood. When his mother brought him to school on his first day, the teacher thanked her and introduced Lucca to the class.

"Boys and girls, this is our new student. His name is Lucca. He has just moved here, so I hope you will all make friends with him and help him get used to our class and our school and our neighborhood."

The teacher, Mr. Fusco, put his arm around Lucca's shoulder and directed him to a seat in the back of the room. As Lucca walked down the aisle, the other children turned to stare at him. He didn't know why they were looking at him. Were his clothes ugly? Was he wearing the wrong shoes? Did he have a bad haircut? Was something wrong with him?

He sat alone at his desk, and no one came over to talk to him. He felt sad and out of place. He wished he were back at his old school, where everyone knew him and everyone was his friend. At this new school, he didn't know anyone.

When the children went out for recess at 10 o'clock, Lucca sat on a bench and watched them play. No one came to talk to him. He felt as if he wanted to cry, but he didn't want anyone to think he was a baby.

What did he have to do to make some friends in his new school? What did he have to do to be accepted?

a. Tell the story about the new boy, Lucca, in your own words.
b. What can you tell about Lucca? What does the story tell you about him?
c. Why do you suppose it is so hard for a new student to make friends in a new school? What explains it? What are your ideas about it?
d. What do you suppose Lucca should do to help him make some new friends? What are your ideas about it? Of all the ideas you can think of, which one do you think is the best idea?

12. *Big idea: What should you do when you are responsible for finishing your chores, but your friends are calling and waiting outside for you?*

"Christa, your room is a mess. I've told you a dozen times to clean up your room. So now get upstairs and get that room cleaned up. You've got toys and books lying all over the floor and your clothes are in a pile on the bed. That is *no* way to keep your room."

Christa felt bad. She had been meaning to get her room cleaned up before this, but there were so many other things she wanted to do first. She had been putting it off and putting it off and putting it off until—she had to agree with her mom: Her room was a big mess.

"But Mom," Christa said, "I promised I would play soccer with the team this afternoon. They *need* me! I'm an important player. I can do my room later."

Christa's mom was angry now. "No way, Christa. You keep promising to do your room and you keep putting it off. And now you want to do the same thing—go out and play ball and leave the room in a mess. No way. You have to do your room first. And no more excuses. Now I'm going off to the market and when I get back, I want to see that room spic and span."

And Christa's mom shut the front door with a slam and left Christa to her job.

She opened the door to her room, and her mom was right. It was a mess. But from the window, she could hear her teammates calling, "Hey, Christa. C'mon down. Hurry up. We're waiting for you."

Christa thought about it. She could sneak off to the game with her friends and do her room afterward. Or she could skip out on the game and get the room cleaned up before her mother got home. She really wanted to go out with her team. But she knew her mother would be furious. So what should she do?

   a. Tell the story about Christa in your own words.
   b. What do know about Christa? What kind of girl is she? What does the story tell you about her?
   c. Is it hard to choose between what you want to do and what your mom tells you to do? What do you think about that?
   d. What should Crista do now? If you were her best friend, what would you tell her?

13. *Big idea: Is it better to follow the crowd or to go your own way?*

Hazel liked to hang out with a group of her friends. They did not always do the kind of things that Hazel liked or thought was good. But she wanted to belong to the group. She did not want to be on her own, with no friends. Wasn't it better to be hanging out with a group of girls, even though you didn't always approve of what they did, instead of having no friends?

After school that day, Hazel and her friends started out for the Dollar Store on Denman Street. Hazel's mother would not have wanted her to go there. Her mom didn't like her to go too far from home. But Hazel wanted to be with her group. So sometimes she had to do things that her mother didn't want her to do.

The girls thought it would be fun to go into the Dollar Store and pick up a few things and put them in their pockets and then dash away, before the owner could catch them. "How about it, Hazel? Let's go!"

Hazel stood back from the group. Should she go with them? She knew that taking things was stealing. That was wrong. But she didn't want to leave her friends. And what if they got caught? What would her mother say?

   a. Tell the story about Hazel in your own words.
   b. What can you tell about Hazel? What kind of girl is she?
   c. What was Hazel's dilemma? What was important to her?
   d. What should Hazel do? If you were her best friend, what would you tell her?

14. Big idea: Should you make time for someone in need when you are busy?

Larissa needed some help. She had just fallen down and hurt her knee. It wasn't bleeding, but it was painful for her to stand up and walk. A girl who lived down the block from her was passing by on the other side of the street. Larissa called out to her: "Hey, Eva. Can you come over here? I fell and hurt my knee. Can you help me get home?"

Eva walked quickly by. She was in a hurry to get to the playground where all her friends were waiting. They were on a volleyball team, and Eva was already late. She knew that her teammates would be angry. Maybe they would tell her that because of her lateness, she would be taken off the team.

Eva wanted to help Larissa. But she didn't want to take the chance of being forced off the team because of her lateness. Anyhow, Larissa's knee didn't look too bad. Maybe someone else would come along and help her.

    a. Tell the story about Larissa and Eva in your own words.
    b. What was Eva's dilemma? What, in your opinion, was important to her?
    c. If you were Eva's friend, what would you tell her to do?

15. Big idea: Should you lend something precious to you when you are worried about its safe return?

Pham was so excited. His uncle had given him a hockey card that was signed by his favorite hockey player. What a gift! He wanted to take the card to school and show it to his friends. But his father said that the card was very precious and that he should not take it to school. It might get lost. He should leave the card at home and keep it in a safe place.

Pham knew his father was right. But he wanted to show the card off. He really wanted his friends to be jealous! How would his friends know if he left the card at home? They would never believe him if he only told them about the card and didn't show it off.

So he secretly tucked the card into his backpack and took it to school with him. In the playground, he took the card out to show his friends. The boys all gathered around him, and they were so excited. They wished they had a signed card too. "How did you get that?" they asked. Pham told them that his uncle knew some of the hockey players, and he was able to get the card signed for him.

Pham's best friend, Gabor, asked him if he could borrow the card to take it to his class and show it to his own classmates. Pham didn't want to lend his friend the card. But he didn't want to disappoint Gabor either. What should Pham do? (Adapted with permission from Eileen Hood's *The Hockey Card*)

a. Tell the story about Pham and his hockey card in your own words.
   b. What, in your opinion, can you tell about Pham?
   c. What, in your opinion, can you tell about Gabor?
   d. What do you think Pham should do? If you were his friend, what would you tell him?

16. *Big idea: Is it fun to play a trick to fool someone?*

Sami was a new boy in grade 2 and so far, he had no friends in the class. But he wanted very much to be a part of this new class, this new school, and this new neighborhood. He and his family had just come from another country and were trying to get settled into their new lives. But it was hard.

The other boys in the class made fun of him during recess. They made fun of his clothes and his accent. They didn't want him in their play groups. Sami stood alone, watching them play. He hadn't realized that it would be so hard to make friends in his new life.

Nick was watching Sami, as he and a few of his classmates were talking. "Hey," Nick said. "Let's play a trick on Sami. Wouldn't that be fun?"

The other boys giggled and said, "Yeah, let's do it."

"Okay," Nick said. "Let's pretend that we are inviting him after school to play ball. Then, when he arrives at the field, no one will be there. Wouldn't that be cool?"

Charlie looked at Nick and at the other boys. He looked mad. "I don't think that's funny. I don't think it's cool to play a trick on Sami. I think that's wrong."

Nick was angry. "You have to be such a wuss, Charlie. If you don't want to be a part of our gang, get lost."

Charlie stood there and didn't know what to do. Should he stay with his group or walk away? He knew that it would be wrong to play a trick on Sami, but he didn't want to lose the friendship of his group. What should he do?

   a. Tell the story about Sami, Nick, and Charlie in your own words.
   b. What can you tell about Sami? What can you tell about Nick? What can you tell about Charlie?
   c. What do you think Sami might do in order to make some friends? How does a new boy go about doing that?
   d. What do you think Charlie should do now? If you were his best friend, what would you tell him?

17. *Big idea: What should a teacher do when the children don't want a certain child in their group?*

Mrs. Burke taught a grade 2 class. She was a good teacher, and her students liked her very much. She did a lot of projects with the class, and they went on many field trips.

In Mrs. Burke's class, the children did a lot of group work. Mrs. Burke liked them to choose the children they wanted to work with, because Mrs. Burke wanted the children to make their own choices when they were working on class projects.

This week, the project the class was working on was dinosaurs. The children were very excited. What is it about dinosaurs that is so fascinating?

"Okay, boys and girls," said Mrs. Burke. "It's time for us to choose your working groups. I'm going to put these titles on the whiteboard, and then you can choose which group you want to join."

Mrs. Burke put five columns on the board, with the following titles: Tyrannosaurus, Stegosaurus, Triceratops, Brachiosaurus, Velociraptor.

"Okay. Now who would like to be in the Tyrannosaurus group?" she asked. And many hands flew up in the air. Mrs. Burke picked five children and put their names on the board for the Tyrannosaurus group.

"Now, who would like to be in the Stegosaurus group?" Mrs. Burke did the same thing and listed the children's names.

She continued in the same way until all the children's names were under each of the dinosaur names.

"Now, that's done," said Mrs. Burke.

But then a few hands went up, and Mrs. Burke said, "Some of you have some questions?" She called on Lenny.

Lenny said, "We're in the Brachiosaurus group and want to change groups . . . because Annette is in our group and we don't want to work with her. She's stupid and she smells bad."

Uh, oh. What was Mrs. Burke going to do about that? What's the right thing for her to do?

   a. Tell the story about Mrs. Burke's class in your own words.
   b. What can you tell about why the children like Mrs. Burke so much?
   c. What can you tell about Annette? What can you tell about Lenny?
   d. What should Mrs. Burke do now?
   e. If she decided to put it to a vote in her class, how would you vote? What would be the right thing to do?

18. *Big idea: What do you say to a girl who is always bragging and lying?*

"Uh, oh! Here she comes again." Minh and her friend Julie saw Evaline coming down the block, and they didn't know whether to stay there or run and hide. "I don't want to have to hear her lies all over again. She's always bragging and telling things that are not true."

But they sat there on the bench and waited. And Evaline came over to them and said, "Hey, you guys. You know what my mother just got me? It's a new dress with ruffles, and it's made of silk. And it cost a hundred dollars. I'm going to a fancy party, and I will be wearing it with my new shoes. They have diamond buckles." Evaline couldn't stop bragging about her new outfit.

But Minh and Julie just stared at her. They didn't know if *this* time Evaline was really telling the truth or whether she was just bragging and lying again.

What should Minh and Julie say to Evaline? What would be the right thing to say?

    a. Tell the story about Minh, Julie, and Evaline in your own words.
    b. What can you tell about Minh and Julie?
    c. What can you tell about Evaline?
    d. What should Minh and Julie say to Evaline? What would be the right thing to say?

19. *Big idea: Is it okay to make fun of a classmate who is not very smart?*

Gary had a hard time in school. He tried very hard, but learning new stuff was a big challenge for him. When he had his turn to read to the group, he stumbled on the easiest words and had to have help from the teacher. When he got his papers back with his arithmetic homework, his papers were full of the teacher's red marks for mistakes he had made. Gary felt that there was something bad about him. Why was it so hard for him to learn what the other kids found so easy? Why didn't his brain work as well as the other children's? He was so ashamed, because he felt he was so slow and so stupid.

The other boys thought it was cool to make fun of Gary. When they were out of the classroom and the teacher was not listening, they would call him names and ridicule him. "Hey stupid! Hey, you moron! Hey, you dork!" And when they did that, Gary felt worse than ever.

So when Benny came to pick up his brother, Clem, after school, and asked him, "Who's the dumbest boy in your class?" Clem didn't know what to answer. He knew that making fun of Gary was not kind. He didn't want to be a part of the boys' group that called him names. But should he tell his brother Benny what he really felt about Gary? Or should he pretend that he didn't know? What's the right thing to do?

    a. Tell the story about Gary in your own words.
    b. What can you tell about Gary?
    c. What can you tell about Clem?

d. What should Clem tell his brother Benny? What is the right thing to do?

20. Big idea: *What should a new girl from a foreign country do when she is ashamed of how her mother looks?*

Aisha and her family had just come to their new country. Everything here was different—so different—from where they lived in Tunisia. Aisha and her family were so happy to be in their new home, but it was hard to get adjusted to all the new ways of this very different world.

It didn't take Aisha long to become a part of her new group in school. The children were happy to have her join them, and many of them took special care to be nice to her and show her what she needed to do with her schoolwork. Aisha soon stopped wearing her old Tunisian clothes, and thanks to the social services in the neighborhood, she was able to get some new clothes that were more like the clothes that her American friends were wearing. It didn't take Aisha long to believe that what she had left behind in Tunisia was not as nice, not as modern, and not as cool as what she now had in America.

So when Aisha was walking home from school with some of her new friends and saw her mother, who was dressed in the clothes of her old country, Aisha was ashamed. And when her mother called out to her, and her friends said, "Who is that lady who is calling you, Aisha?" she said, "I don't know. She must be making a mistake. I don't know her."

   a. Tell the story about Aisha in your own words.
   b. What do you know about Aisha?
   c. What can you tell about the girls in Aisha's class?
   d. Why do you suppose Aisha said that about her mother? What are your thoughts about that?
   e. What do you think Aisha should have done instead of pretending she didn't know her mother? Why do you think that was wrong?

21. Big idea: *Should you stick up for another boy when the bullies could pick on you as well?*

There were three boys who were always picking on Benno. It's true that Benno was not the teacher's favorite. He was not a good student. He was not handsome. He didn't get his work done on time. The teacher had to scold him a lot. And when she did that, Benno put down his head and cried. But he couldn't help being slow. School stuff was just too hard for him.

In the school yard at recess, the three boys from Benno's class thought it was great to make fun of him. They called him names. "Bennooooo Dumbo, you are such a crybaby. You are such a loser." Their words were harsh and cruel. Mark, Curtis, and Spencer made a circle around him and continued to bully him. Benno couldn't get out of the circle. He just sat down on the ground and cried. "Crybaby. Crybaby!" the boys shouted and laughed. The more they did this, the more Benno cried.

Was there anyone on the playground who would help Benno? Was there a boy or girl who would stand up to those bullies and get Benno away from them?

Kai thought about it. If he stepped in to help Benno, wouldn't the boys then start to pick on him as well? But how could he just stand by and watch when he knew that was wrong?

   a. Tell the story about Benno and the bullies in your own words.
   b. What can you tell about Benno?
   c. What can you tell about Mark, Curtis, and Spencer?
   d. What was Kai's dilemma?
   e. What should Kai do? What would you do if you were in Kai's place?

22. *Big Idea: Should we keep wild animals in the zoo or set them free?*

Mrs. Baker's class had just come from a visit to the zoo, where they were able to observe lions, tigers, and other wild, captured animals in their cages. Some of the children, in a discussion after the zoo visit, were talking about whether it was fair to the animals to capture them and keep them in cages.

Some children said it was good that the animals in zoos were safe and got fed every day. If they were free, they could be in danger from other animals, and they might be hungry if they couldn't find food. Other children said that it was better to be free and hungry than have food and be locked up in a cage.

Mrs. Baker asked them, "What's the right thing to do? Should we close down all the zoos and let the animals return to their native homes? Or should we keep them safe, in zoos, where they are protected and fed? What are your ideas?"

   a. Tell the story about Mrs. Baker's class visit to the zoo.
   b. What are your own ideas about keeping animals in zoos?
   c. What do you think? Should animals be kept in zoos where they are caged but fed and safe?
   d. Or should they be left free and in the wild?

INVITING CHILDREN'S STORIES ABOUT THEIR OWN DILEMMAS

There are, more than likely, many times when children in the early childhood years are faced with their own personal dilemmas, times when they were called on to make decisions that have moral underpinnings, when they are pulled by two opposing motivations to act.

When there is trust in the adult-child relationship, children may feel more inclined to talk about such events—and they might be invited to do so as an alternative to, or in addition to, using stories, films, and mini-cases. In fact, the mini-cases and films are likely to give rise to more personal disclosures.

Invitations to discuss such events are better done in a small group, where the group members can get support from each other and from the similar experiences of others. Once again, parents or teachers who engage in this context are cautioned to maintain their nonjudgmental stance in words used, tone of voice, and facial expression. If children are to be allowed to disclose freely and openly, they are not likely to do so in an environment where they are going to be judged. This gets easier for an adult to do with practice; but it is not easy when children are speaking on an issue that is morally reprehensible to the adult. There are no hard and fast rules for learning how to maintain a neutral stance. But for these discussions to be effective, it is nonnegotiable.

A list of prompts is offered below to encourage the children to talk about their own issues. These can serve as a basis for beginning other discussions, or they can be used as discussion leaders.

Once the children have volunteered their stories, follow-up questions may be asked that address the moral issues, enable thoughtful consideration of the choices being made, examine why those choices seemed important at the time, and examine what was known about the people in the situation and, of course, what was the right thing to do. These questions are discussed in the following chapter.

- I hurt my friend's feelings, and I was sorry.
- My mother wanted me to clean up my room, but my friends were calling me to come and play.
- My younger brother wanted me to take him out to play, but he's a pest and I didn't want him hanging around with me and my friends.
- My father said I needed to practice the piano for an hour every day. But how can I tell him that I hate piano lessons?
- I spilled the finger paint on the kitchen floor, and I blamed it on my brother.
- My father said I should put the light out at 8:30 and go to sleep. But I had a flashlight and could use it to read my book under the covers. I really wanted to finish that story.
- My mother said I should go with her to visit my grandmother. But my grandma is sick, and I hate to go there.
- I don't think it's fair to have homework. We work hard enough in school and need time to play at home.

- Why do I have to eat my broccoli? I can give it to the dog when my mother isn't looking.
- I don't see why I have to practice my handwriting. Nobody writes anymore. We all use computers.
- My uncle gave me $10.00 for my birthday. My friend, Carlos, said I should share it with him and we could get some pizza together.
- Cicely asked to be my friend. But I don't like her. She lies all the time.
- My grandmother said I should be a good boy. What does that mean?
- I think it's okay to tell a little lie if no one is going to be hurt by it.
- I got a bad mark on my math paper, and I'm afraid to take it home to show it to my father.
- I saw Robbie take the candy bar from Susie's backpack. Should I tell on him?
- My mother said I have to wear my sweater, but I'm not cold. I can take it off when she's not looking.
- My grandmother's cookies are terrible. I think she doesn't put enough sugar in them. So when she offers me a cookie, what can I say to her?
- Fred wants me to go on the roller coaster ride with him. But I'm afraid. If I tell him that, he will call me a sissy.
- My favorite programs are cartoons. My sister says that cartoons are for babies and that I should "grow up."
- If you were the teacher, what would you change about this class?
- I know I should recycle those cans, but it's easier for me to just throw them in the garbage.
- I think it's okay to make fun of someone who is very fat, because the reason they are fat is because they eat too much and they shouldn't do that.
- Malcolm wanted to be class president, but he didn't get enough votes. He was the best and smartest and should have gotten elected.
- Our team lost the game, but I think it's because the other guys didn't play fair.
- My dad says that I shouldn't spend too much time on the computer playing games, that it is bad for my brain. But I think he's just making that up.
- Those kids who have Facebook pages should not spend so much time on Facebook. It's a waste of time.
- Mindy won't wear any clothes that don't have designer labels. I think she's stuck up.
- Why are some kids so worried about how they look? What does how you look have to do with anything?

- If I'm putting a picture of myself on Facebook, I'm going to do some photoshopping to make myself look more beautiful/handsome.

CHILDREN'S BOOKS AND STORIES

Children's literature offers a treasure trove of stories that center on moral dilemmas—and a quick trip to the school or local library will provide the searching adult with an array of sources to read to and/or with the children. Literature is a prime source not only because the stories are rich, engaging, and inventive but also because they reveal that other children in the wide world face similar moral dilemmas to those of the children sitting at one's knee. Looking at the dilemmas of others, and discovering how others face them and make choices, is not only edifying but also reassuring.

Aesop, a Greek fabulist who wrote in the fourth century BCE, was, arguably, the first storywriter to give us tales with moral overtones. In fact, *Aesop's Fables* endures today, in many updated forms, some 2,500 years later. So in searching the literature, one could easily begin with Aesop, selecting tales that have relevance for the lives of children today. In the whole collection, which is housed in the Library of Congress, for example, there are 656 fables. However, one need not make a trip to Washington, DC, to get them. The Internet as well as local and school libraries are much more accessible resources.

The Library of Congress, however, has the most complete list, and it can be accessed at read.gov. Additional descriptions of the fables can be found at taleswithmorals.com, and clicking on a given title will bring up a literate summary of the tale, highlighting the moral dilemma. In other words, the Internet is a huge source of materials at one's fingertips. Or as some high-tech wonk once said, "Google is your friend."

The list of books included below make up only a small portion of what is available in the vast world of children's literature. But the adult should be wary, as some stories, rather than opening up lines of inquiry about "the right thing to do," instead preach moral certitudes. These are not bad or wrong, but they are inappropriate for engaging children in thinking and open-ended inquiry where they are called on to make up their own minds.

Professor Meguido Zola, who is one expert in the field of children's literature, suggests *The Big Orange Splot*, by Daniel Manus Pinkwater, a tale about conformism and individualism, as well as the four Frog and Toad books, "golden oldies" by Arnold Lobel. Happily, these four books are available online.

Dr. Dolores Van Der Wey, doing research with young children in Surrey, British Columbia, Canada, has made use of what is referred to as

First Nations (indigenous) literature in Canada. She has used the following books in her discussions with children about moral issues:

A Salmon for Simon, by Betty Waterton. A First Nations boy has cast his line into the water, hoping to catch a salmon. As he sits there and waits, an eagle drops a salmon into a tidal pool. Simon is torn between his sympathy for the fish and his hope to bring a salmon home for dinner.

Pettranella, by Betty Waterton. Pettranella is moving to a new homestead. Her grandmother gives her a packet of seeds to plant in her new home. But when she arrives, she finds that the seeds have been lost.

Mary of Mile 18, by Ann Blades. Mary has found a wolf pup, but her parents tell her she can't keep it as a pet.

A Promise Is a Promise, by Robert Munsch. Allashua wants to go fishing on the sea ice, but her parents have forbidden her to go.

Six Darn Cows, by Margaret Laurence. Two children are responsible for looking after the family's six cows. To their dismay, they find that the gate has been left open and the cows are gone!

Too Small, by Ann Blades. Two children have had to move to a smaller house, and they are complaining that the house is too small. How do they learn to appreciate the size that they have been given?

Back to the Cabin, by Ann Blades. Two boys have to go with their parents to a cabin in the woods for the summer. But there's no TV, no video games, no Internet—how are they going to learn to live without their favorite toys?

Shi-Shi-Etko, by Nicola Campbell. Young Shi-shi-etko is being forced to leave her family and attend the residential school. How is she going to endure this hardship?

Beaver Steals Fire, by the Salish and Kootenai Tribes. When fire belonged only to animals who lived in the sky world, Coyote and his friends make a plan to steal fire for themselves.

Recent collections of children's literature deal with more sensitive issues like divorce, autism, broken families, illness, death—and the Luria Library at Santa Barbara City College has a list, with descriptions of the books. See http://library.sbcc.edu/findsearch/research-guides/childrens-literature-picture-books-on-social-and-personal-issues-in-the-luria-library-collection/. The list includes the following:

The Giving Tree, by Shel Silverstein. The relationship between a boy and a tree: The tree is "giving," and the boy is a "taker."

Big Sister and Little Sister, by Charlotte Zolotow. A big sister is excessive in her control over her little sister, trying to teach her what to do.

Junie B. Jones Is (Almost) a Flower Girl, by Barbara Park. Junie wanted so much to be the flower girl at her aunt's wedding, but she wasn't chosen.

Ella Enchanted, by Gail Carson Levine. Ella's fairy godmother gives her the magical gift that requires her to obey everything she is asked to do. Is this a gift or a curse?

Love You Forever, by Robert Munsch. Even though the boy's behavior is very naughty, his mother continues to shower him with love.

Frederick, by Leo Lionni. Related to Aesop's tale, this story is about a field mouse who does not participate in the family's preparations of gathering food for the long winter.

Matilda, by Roald Dahl. This book was not a "winner" with some adults, as it is a story about a good, smart child who triumphs over evil adults.

The Great Blueness, by Arnold Lobel. When all the world had no colors and everything was gray or black or white, the people were excited when a wizard came and colored everything blue. Now everything in the world was blue. Did that make them happy?

The Paper Bag Princess, by Robert Munsch. Although the princess, who is left without any of her fine clothes and has only a paper bag to wear, defeats the bad dragon and frees her prince from his evil spell, the prince tells her to leave and return only when she looks like a princess.

Mortimer, by Robert Munsch. Mortimer doesn't want to go to bed and uses all kinds of strategies to get his parents to come into his room and tell him to be quiet. What "pretend" behaviors do we use to get attention from others?

No Excuses! by Wayne W. Dyer. Using excuses as rationales for avoiding activities that are challenging is one way to remain "stuck" and disabled. Recognizing such behavior in ourselves is a first step in overcoming the fears that keep us from moving ahead. How does this kind of behavior disable us?

Everyone Matters, by Pat Thomas. Earning respect means valuing the worth of others and treating people equally, no matter how different they are from us. How hard is that to do?

How Full Is Your Bucket? by Tom Rath. A "full bucket" is a metaphor for feeling good about oneself. What do we have to do to fill our bucket so that we feel better about who we are and what we do? What do we do to fill the buckets of our classmates, friends, and family members?

Families Change, by Julie Nelson and Mary Gallagher. When families change, the child in the middle is faced with the need to accommodate to those changes, as, for example, when a new baby is born, when parents divorce, or when there is a new mom or dad. What's the right thing to do when facing those changes?

Oliver Button Is a Sissy, by Tomie de Paola. Some children are different. Oliver doesn't like the things that other boys like. The other boys bully him and call him a sissy. How do you respond to children who are different? What's the right thing to do?

Leo the Late Bloomer, by Robert Krauss. Leo is slower than the other children in everything he does. While the other children can read, write, draw, and speak, Leo is far behind. How do you respond to children like Leo? What's the right thing to do?

Eli's Lie-O-Meter, by Sandra Levins. Eli does know the difference between telling the truth and lying, but it is hard for him to keep from exaggerating and telling lies. How do you respond to Eli? What's the right thing to do?

Yoko, by Rosemary Wells. Yoko is different from the other children in the class. She wears different clothes and she eats different foods for her snacks and her lunch. Some of the other children look at her lunch and say, "Yuck!" They make her feel ashamed of what she is eating.

There is an abundance of children's books and stories that deal with moral issues; the above list is, of course, selective. Using one's favorite search engine or consulting with the school or neighborhood librarian can undoubtedly lead to more books than can be fit into a school year. In other words, there is no dearth of resources that can be used to begin discussions about moral issues in a child's world.

FILMS

Using films or what is available on DVD or streaming services is, perhaps, a more ambitious strategy for generating discussions on moral issues. Yet children do love animated films, and some of these are rich with potential for individual or group discussions. Relatively easy to obtain are productions by the Walt Disney Company—especially those animated films that come from children's favorite stories. A few of these are listed below and the moral issues identified.

Dumbo—An elephant is born with excessively large ears. While he is mocked by others, it turns out that his ears are not impediments but rather benefits that enable him to fly. What's the right thing to do when a person is markedly different from the rest of us?

A Bug's Life—Another film about a "misfit" who turns out to be a hero. Dealing with those who are different is a repeated theme. When children face peers or adults who are different, how do they respond? What's the right thing to do?

Bambi—The story of a young deer growing up in the forest. The moral issue of hunting animals may perhaps be too mature for young children, and teachers are advised to consider this before choosing this longtime favorite film.

Beauty and the Beast—A young prince is turned into a beast because of his selfishness, and he must live out his life until he is released from the curse by the kiss of a beautiful woman. Can we learn to love others who are far from beautiful? Should a person have to pay a penalty of being turned into a beast for his selfish ways?

Cinderella—Three cruel stepsisters make Cinderella's life unbearable. But she gets help from her fairy godmother, who provides her with a gown and slippers so that she can go to the prince's ball. Does kindness pay in the end? Does cruelty pay in the end?

Lambert the Sheepish Lion—A stork delivers a lion cub named Lambert to a flock of sheep by mistake. How does Lambert fit in? How does a person fit in with a group where he is rejected and made to feel as if he doesn't belong?

Pinocchio—The old favorite story of a wooden puppet who told a lot of lies in his desire to become a "real boy." Jiminy Cricket, his conscience, guides him about what is right and wrong. What "cricket" do children use to help them decide what's the right thing to do?

Snow White and the Seven Dwarfs—A wicked stepmother drives young Snow White into the forest, where she is taken in by a group of seven dwarfs. The wicked stepmother is obsessed with being the "most beautiful" in the land, but in that ambition, she is outclassed by Snow White. What is the importance of physical beauty? Why do we put such a high value on how a person looks?

A more extensive list of films available from the Walt Disney Studios can be found on several Internet sites; compilations may be found, for example, on the Internet Movie Database, among them, https://www.imdb.com/list/ls050952391/?sort=list_order,asc&st_dt=&mode=detail&page=2.

Animated films are not the only cinematic resources that center on moral issues. More sophisticated offerings are also available but should be reserved for work with older children. A few classics come to mind: *The Diary of Anne Frank, To Kill a Mockingbird, Sounder, Edward Scissorhands, Free Willy, Charlotte's Web, The Lion King, Willy Wonka and the Chocolate Factory,* and *The Yearling.*

To sum up this lengthy chapter about resources that can initiate discussions about moral issues, it is clear that there is no dearth of options—from mini-cases to issues in the children's lives to books and stories and films to exemplars of children who choose to act for the good of others. For parents and teachers who are choosing from among those resources, it is important to keep in mind the maturity level of the children, their experiences, their immediate needs, their sensitivities, and their relationship with the adults. The bottom line in making choices is, of course, that they be respectful of children and sensitively aware of them as developing persons.

SIX

Putting Moral Behavior Into Action

A Chapter Primarily for Teachers

In these days of "helicopter parenting," it may be perverse to suggest experiences that take young children outside, into the community, on their own. So what is being suggested in this chapter should be taken in light of what is viable in the neighborhood; what is allowable for children, given parental concerns and constraints; and what falls within the limits and limitations of school rules and regulations. In those schools and communities that not only allow such ventures but actually encourage them, the suggestions that follow may give teachers some ideas for engaging children in actively applying their values to the community in which they live.

Most of these suggestions are school-based, but a few of them are applicable to parents.

Not only will such community projects engage children in "doing good" for others but they will also have the effect of reaffirming for children what is means to behave with concern for others—in other words, they will promote the further development of a moral sense.

As a starting point, it is suggested that children first make choices about what they want to do, create plans for how it is to be done, and choose like-minded classmates or a friend with whom to work. This is done a priori, in the classroom, under the supervision and guidance of the teacher, before undertaking the work outside of school. For example, the teacher helps the children to define the project, sets out the parameters of what is to be done, and, in consultation with the children, establishes guidelines for implementation.

If unaccompanied work outside of school is not viable or not appropriate, an adult can stand by to oversee and monitor the situation so that children are never in any kind of danger. Some projects may be carried out in areas in and around the school. Some may be implemented in communities outside the home.

COMMUNITY PROJECTS

Many, but not necessarily all, communities have needs that are unmet and can be attended to even by children in the early childhood years. It is suggested that such needs be identified by the teacher in consultation with the children, a list drawn up, and children given choices for what they would like to undertake. Community outreach work can be done in small groups during school hours, when that kind of work is allowed by the school rules and regulations. Otherwise, outreach projects that children can and should arrange by themselves, with some adult guidance, can be carried out after school. Teachers and/or parents should decide if an adult standing by and acting as a monitor for the children's safety is necessary.

When outreach projects are not within the realm of what is possible in a school or neighborhood, community projects can also be classroom-based. Teachers should feel free to create variations on the suggestions below to suit their own classroom and school mandates.

1. Bake sales to raise money for those in need

Baking cookies or muffins or other kinds of pastries is not only fun but also carries with it learning about reading recipes, measurement, and working cooperatively in groups. Baking in groups can be done in school, or at home—and the conditions can be easily manipulated. What is important is that children identify some community need, which may be for the school library or gymnasium, for some family new to the neighborhood, or for the local library or senior center. The need should be identified first and then decisions made about what is to be baked, where the ingredients will come from, how the baked goods will be sold, and for what prices. How the money will be donated should also be addressed, discussed, and evaluated. Alternatively, the baked goods may simply be donated to a community or senior center.

More than the sense of helping to fill an important need, there is much learning that comes from such an activity.

2. Community car wash

In several suburban communities, signs are raised on weekends offering car washes by students raising money for the special needs of their schools. Is it asking too much that children in the early childhood years undertake a car washing project to raise money for special causes?

There is a tendency among some adults and teachers to underestimate the many ways in which young children can rise to more challenging tasks. While it was surely a special time, a time of great need, and a time when every effort of every person counted, it was not unusual during WWII in London that young children formed groups to collect salvage—paper, iron, steel, and rubber—and they were considered to be making an important contribution to the war effort. In fact, stories about salvage drives were prominent in popular and scholarly histories, depicting how such drives contributed to patriotism and community spirit.

Although children close to us do not face a world at war, the idea of making an important contribution to their community is not above their interests or capabilities. Offering, as a school or class project, to wash cars requires some advance arranging; there must be buckets with soap and water, sponges, a hose and nozzle with a water outlet, clean cloths for drying, and of course, signs that advertise their project. Children involved in a car wash project should be cautioned about proper clothing, and perhaps this activity is better left to the warmer weather.

Since water play is a favorite among young children, volunteers for this project may be easy to acquire. Decisions about how the collected funds will be deployed should be decided before the car wash project is set in motion. Besides the actual washing, there is important learning involved in collecting the money, making change, and deciding, of course, the price of the wash.

3. Collecting and donating used toys, games, and stuffed animals

Many young children of the middle and upper classes are blessed with an abundance of toys and games by doting parents, grandparents, friends, and aunts and uncles. When children outgrow toys and games, many of them are still in good condition. Instead of being stored in attics and backs of closets, they can be collected and given to other children who are less fortunate and less blessed with such largesse.

A drive to collect old and used toys and games, still in good condition, can be initiated; the items can be brought to school and deposited at some collection point. Finding ways to give them away is a second part of the collection project—identifying those in need, locating the places to deposit the toys and games, and ensuring that they find their way to them. Children may be involved in that identification, and care should be taken that no recipient child is made to feel ashamed for the gift he or she is given.

Perhaps the donor children could add a note to the toy, game, or stuffed animal that is to be given away, signifying that this is a gift that is offered with good wishes to the recipient.

4. Putting on a show

Another money raiser that does not require work outside the school is for the children to put on a play, perhaps something original that they create, or even the dramatic acting out of a fairy tale or other story that they enjoy.

Care should be taken that every child who wants a part gets one, that no one is left out of this project. Rehearsals, costuming, and makeup are also rich learning activities, and a schedule of performances can be created as flyers and posted in prominent places, so that anyone from the community may attend. Fees for attendance should be voluntary—people should give what they can—knowing in advance that the money collected will be donated to some important cause. Counting the profits and deciding to whom the money is to be given or how it is to be spent should culminate the project.

5. Collecting used books for donations

Similar to the toys and games collection project, children can also be involved in the gathering of used books that no longer have a place in the family library. These, too, can be collected and placed in some depository in the school. Once gathered, they may be classified according to category—adult books, children's books, fiction, nonfiction, and so forth—which makes it easier to decide to whom the books are to be donated.

There are two ways to dispatch the books in this project. One is to sell them to a used book dealer, collect the money, and donate the money to the school library, the local library, the senior center, the community center, or any other worthwhile organization. Another way is to donate them to a hospital library, a senior center, a community center, a hospice, or any other worthwhile and needy group.

6. Volunteer dog walking

In some communities, there are older and infirm people who are no longer able to care for their pets but who would not dream of giving them up. Help in the form of volunteer dog walking can be undertaken by young children who live in the neighborhood. This project can begin by posting signs in the local market or on the school bulletin board, and children who are interested and able can volunteer to take on such a task. This is a bit more complicated in terms of logistics, but teachers and parents who understand the need can provide guidance and help to children who would be interested in providing this kind of help.

7. Sponsoring recycling drives

One of the more compelling problems facing planet earth is, undoubtedly, global warming. Despite the few naysayers, what is happening on a global scale is both terrifying and in need of our attention and concern. It is not farfetched for children, even in the early childhood years, to be reminded that the earth and its oceans are fragile and need our care.

One of the ways in which children can add to the efforts to help redress waste and pollution is by involving them in recycling projects. At the outset, they need to understand the reasons for the need to recycle and reuse—that, for example, waste has a huge negative impact on the natural environment and that when we recycle, we help to reduce the pollution caused by waste. The information doesn't have to be too alarming for them, nor does it have to be overly complicated. Like the children who were involved in gathering scrap for the war effort, children today can understand a few simple concepts that will give them real reasons for participating in recycling efforts.

This kind of project can be done on a personal basis, and it can be done in small groups. Beginning with some guidelines for what and how, teachers and parents can initiate these efforts. Identification of where recycling depots exist, how to move the recycled material to the depots, and what different depots accept should begin the project.

Generating children's interest in the need for recycling has a larger payoff in terms of making them more aware of every individual's role in the protection and care of our planet.

8. Community farm in the schoolyard

Alice Waters, the doyenne of haute cuisine and pioneer in the use of local, fresh, organic food in her world-famous restaurant, has made a second career for herself by volunteering in local schools in Berkeley, California, and helping children to create their own school yard gardens. Her "Edible Schoolyard Project" involves students in all aspects of farming and gardening, including preparing, serving, and eating food "as a means of awakening their senses and encouraging awareness and appreciation of the transformative values of nourishment, community and stewardship of the land" (Waters, 1999).

The Edible Schoolyard project, begun in Waters's home territory of Berkeley, California, put down its roots in the King Middle School, which now serves as a model for other Edible Schoolyard programs that are being cultivated around the United States. According to recent sources, there are now Edible Schoolyard programs in New Orleans, Los Angeles, San Francisco, and Brooklyn.

There is, of course, much learning that comes from students' involvement in creating their own gardens—beyond the most obvious of understanding and applying principles of planting, growing, and harvesting. Math, science, and reading are learning activities that are embedded in such undertaking.

Not every school yard can easily accommodate an edible garden, but those schools with cement and concrete yards can use planting boxes, which can be built in shop classes or in home shops and donated to the project by parents. Some schools fortunate enough to have a vacant lot behind or adjacent to the school have viable options, provided permission is sought and granted for the use of the space.

This classroom or school-based project does not necessarily have to follow the parameters and design of Waters's Edible Schoolyard Project, which is supported by her foundation and includes, for example, learning about cycles, seasonality, sustainability, the personal impact of food choices, and wellness through healthy food choices. It can be less broad and extensive, to include primarily studies of what to plant, the nature of the soil used, what the soil requires for fertilization, how to plant, how to ensure that the plants thrive, care for the garden during growing times, watering, and later on, harvesting.

If possible, the project can also extend to cooking and eating what is grown, choosing recipes, and organizing a lunch with homegrown food.

There is much to be gained and much to be learned in such a project, but the extent and nature of it are perhaps best suited to the more intrepid teacher, who may see this as a large umbrella undertaking that may absorb a good deal of class time.

But clearly, the benefits of such a project are far-reaching and extend beyond the increased awareness of wholesome, organic food, care for a garden, and the overall sense of wellness through food choice into giving children a greater appreciation of how food is grown and what it means to have a sustainable garden in one's backyard.

Materials about the Edible Schoolyard Project can be easily obtained from its website: https://edibleschoolyard.org.

9. Clean up litter project

Driving along Interstate 5 going north or south, it is possible to see highway signs at the side of the road indicating which group or organization is responsible for cleaning up the litter along the highway. So cleaning up litter campaigns are not necessarily school-based; they can extend to larger organizations that also serve a community need.

It is unfortunate, but an unhappy fact of life is that some people discard their pop cans, cigarette and candy wrappers, paper plates, and other detritus not only along the highways, tossed out of cars, but along sidewalks, wilderness paths, and even—alas—in the local parks and playgrounds.

A clean up litter project is one that is easily done by children in the early childhood years. Some advance preparation is warranted, as it is in all the other outreach projects.

At the very first, children should begin with a knowledge and appreciation of why litter is not only unsightly but also hazardous—an awareness of how litter despoils the environment and contributes to environmental pollution. There is danger in litter on wilderness trails; for example, animals may ingest it and die. Litter may end up in rivers and lakes and oceans, corrupting and polluting them. As more and more people litter, the impact of nonbiodegradable waste on the infrastructure of the planet is extensive. According to several resources about the environment, "litter programs are critically relevant for future generations."

This may be a project that is not for the more timid, because it involves doing things that might be unappetizing. Picking up someone else's garbage—ugh!

If children are to participate in such a venture, they should have adequate protection: rubber gloves, for example, and a caution to *not* touch any of the litter with their hands. A hand sanitizer is also a good idea. A pronged stick that enables them to pick up pieces of litter without touching it and a big, reusable collection bag in which to contain it are simple but adequate supplies.

The benefits of such a cleanup program are not only that it makes our world more beautiful and less ugly—not a small reward—but that it also makes children more aware of the need for environmental care and more sensitive to becoming more responsible about waste disposal. No small potatoes.

10. One-on-One Tutoring

It may be a stretch to think that young children in the primary grades can help others who are younger and perhaps less academically capable. But experience with young children has given many teachers evidence that even primary graders can extend a "teaching" hand to others.

There are multiple payoffs for this kind of one-on-one tutoring. First, it gives children a chance to experience the benefits of helping others—an ego boost and a sense of empowerment. Second, the data suggest that there is learning for the tutor as well as for the child on the other side of the log (Logan & Mayer, 2013). Odd as it may sound, there is an increase in skill to the tutor, as one learns more about what he or she is teaching from teaching others. Third, there is the satisfaction that one gets from knowing that one can make a difference to the lives of others.

These one-on-one tutoring sessions can occur within the scope of a school day—with time allocated for such sessions. Children at home can read to younger brothers and sisters or to neighboring children or to neighbors and family members who are infirm and would like the company. Diane, an immigrant from China, enjoys having her three-year-old granddaughter instruct her in proper English pronunciation.

It is a given that children should volunteer for such service if and when the opportunity to participate in tutoring others is an option. Parents, of course, must give their approval, whether the tutoring is done in school or from a home base. Language arts is the area in which such one-on-one tutoring can most fruitfully occur.

EXTRACTING MEANING FROM EXPERIENCE

The various outreach projects described above, in which children can provide help to others, to the community, or to the school, are only a beginning list. Teachers and parents who are vastly more creative will likely think of many other opportunities for children to help others, to "put moral behavior into action."

Because not all experiences are "equal" in terms of which have moral dimensions, what is chosen should at least have, at the bottom line, a way for the experience to make the community a better place and/or contribute to the welfare and well-being of others. What's important is that children develop a sense of what it means to care for others and for their world, and to find benefits to themselves in doing that.

Such experiences can be heightened by a follow-up discussion that focuses on what the children have done, how they have made their contributions, and what has been distilled from that participation. In other words, while the experience itself can "stand on its own feet" as having meaning in the children's lives, it is enriched by a discussion that enables the extraction of the deeper meanings—the "squeezing out" of the big ideas in and around the experience and how the participation in the experience has benefited the children both cognitively and emotionally.

Such a discussion centers on how we use the experience to inform our lives and deepen our understanding and appreciation; how it shapes our values, ideas, and attitudes; and what potential it has for changing our thinking and behavior for the better.

To extract meaning from experience requires the application of student thinking, from reflecting on what they have done, to meaning making, to wisdom. This kind of thoughtful, critical analysis of the experience helps students to develop insight, see the experience from new perspectives. Because an experience in itself does not necessarily lead to informed understanding, children need to work at the process, applying intelligent habits of mind to benefit more from the lived experience.

Chapter 7 provides a detailed discussion of how moral issues are examined, using reflective responses and higher order questions, in an absence of moral judgment by the discussion leader. But as an introduction to that chapter, and to provide a concrete example of how the adult leads a discussion to extract meaning from experience, the following example is offered.

The grade 2 children have participated in an outreach project, working in groups of four, to collect used children's books that they planned to contribute to a local hospital library. Their work began with creating posters that they drew for display, placing them in strategic places around the school, indicating when the collection would occur, to whom the donated books would be given, and why the project was important. Permission for collecting books from children in other classes was sought and given by the principal.

On the appointed day, the groups visited the various classrooms to collect the books. Together they managed to gather over a hundred children's books, which they bundled and arranged to be taken to the children's ward of the local hospital. Their teacher, Ms. Alper, has now gathered the children together to "debrief" their experiences with this project. What follows is a prototypical transcript of their discussion.

Ms. Alper: You have finished your project and collected over a hundred books. Now that we are sitting together, I'd like you to summarize for me how you began this project and what you did.

Damon: It was good. We got a lot of books.

Ms. Alper: Thank you Damon. You were pleased with what you did.

Damon: Yeah. It was fun too. And we're going to take the books over to the hospital for the sick kids.

Ms. Alper: The work is not finished. You're going to take the books to the hospital.

Damon: Yeah.

Ms. Alper: I wonder if someone can tell me how this big project started.

Claudia: We decided about what we were going to do. We wanted to do something to help somebody. Then we made some posters and put them up all over the school.

Ms. Alper: The first thing you did was to decide on the kind of project you wanted to do. You wanted to do something to help others. You chose to collect used books from the other classes in the school to donate to the children's ward in the hospital. And you made some posters and put them up all over the school.

Claudia: Yeah. My poster went to the library. Sasha and I worked on the poster.

Ms. Alper: What was it about your poster, do you think, that made the other students interested in giving up their old books?

Claudia: (*Is quiet and doesn't respond.*)

Ms. Alper: That's a hard question. Let me try to say it a different way. The way you made your poster made children want to give their books to you.

Claudia: Yeah. It had nice colors so they would want to read what it said.

Ms. Alper: The colors made it attractive. That's what caught the people's attention.

Claudia: Yeah. And we gave the information too. Like when we were going to collect the books and where we were going to give them.

Ms. Alper: It was helpful to give the information so that the children would know when to bring their books and why it was important to make the donation.

Claudia: Yeah. And we got a *lot* of books!

Ms. Alper: You were pleased to see how many books you were able to collect. I wonder if anyone can tell me about how the children in the other classes responded to your appeal to donate books.

Teacher waits . . .

La Toya: I went to the grade 6 classes. A lot of them gave me books. But some didn't.

Ms. Alper: Not all of the children in the grade 6 classes gave you books for your collection. Some didn't give any.

La Toya: I could see some of them laughing. They didn't think what we were doing was important.

Ms. Alper: Some children remembered to bring books from home and gave them to you. Other children not only didn't bring books but they didn't take you seriously.

La Toya: They were making fun of us. Some of the big boys. The teacher had to scold them. They said that the books weren't going to make sick people get well.

Ms. Alper: I can see from the look on your face that that made you upset. The boys didn't understand that giving books to the children in the hospital was not to make them get well but to cheer them up.

La Toya: Yeah. To cheer them up. And that's important too. You know if they didn't want to give us their old books, they didn't have to give them. But they didn't have to make fun of us.

Ms. Alper: It was upsetting to see that some of the big boys were laughing at you. Perhaps they didn't care about the children in the hospital getting those books.

La Toya: If they were sick and in the hospital, they would care. They would be happy to get the books. They would understand that books can cheer you up when you are feeling sick.

Ms. Alper: The grade 6 boys didn't seem to care about the children in the hospital and how the books would make them feel.

La Toya: If I was in the hospital and I got some books to read, that would make me happy. I could get better quicker.

Ms. Alper: The big boys didn't understand that getting some books from what you children had collected might make the sick children feel happier. They didn't understand that this was a nice thing to do for children who were sick.

La Toya: I don't care about them. We did a good thing, and they are just stupid.

Ms. Alper: You are really mad at them for how they laughed at what you were doing. But you know you and your classmates did a very good thing for children in the hospital. I wonder, now, what anyone can tell me about what it means to you to do this kind of project to help other people.

Zeb: I think it means that it makes you feel good to do something nice for someone else.

Ms. Alper: When you do something nice for someone else, you feel good about what you did.

Zeb: Yeah. Like when you do something bad to someone else, you feel bad after you did it.

Ms. Alper: Doing something good for others makes you feel good and maybe proud of yourself. And when you hurt or harm someone, you feel bad. Your conscience tells you that it wasn't a nice thing to do.

Zeb: Yeah. That's right. So when you do something nice for others, and you feel good yourself, it's good for you and it's good for the other person too.

Ms. Alper: You get a double reward, helping someone else is good for them and it's good for you too.

Zeb: Yeah. (*Smiles shyly.*)

Ms. Alper: I want to thank all of you for sharing your ideas and I want to thank you, too, for all the hard work you did to collect books for the children in the hospital ward. We are going to have to decide how we are going to take them over there. That's the next project. I wonder if anyone has any ideas about that?

JOURNALS

Some researchers have described journaling as a powerful tool for becoming more aware of one's own feelings, wishes, expectations, thoughts, and behavior; in other words, it can be a therapeutic process that enables the writer to become more aware of who he or she is and what motivates his and her behavior.

According to a report in *The New York Times*, writing in a journal has additional benefits. As unlikely as it sounds, journaling can lead to better sleep, a stronger immune system, more self-confidence, and a higher IQ (Phelan, 2018). James W. Pennebaker, a social psychologist, has added that keeping a journal helps to organize events in our mind, helps us make sense of trauma, improves our mood, and helps us perform better (Phelan, 2018).

It is unlikely that this medium will work for kindergarten, for obvious reasons. But beginning in grade 1, children can be encouraged to keep a journal and, using emergent spelling, will be able to express what is going on in their heads and hearts.

Journal writing can be open-ended; that is, time is set aside every day for an entry, and children may write whatever is on their minds. Or it can begin with prompts—topics and ideas suggested by the teacher or parent to focus writing in a particular area. Since getting at a child's ideas and feelings about moral issues is the primary focus of these activities, it is probably a good idea to use both forms—open-ended writing without prompts as well as writing with prompts.

There are several important aspects to journal writing that make it a successful and valuable strategy. First, the teacher or parent never, ever, marks, judges, or evaluates what the child has written, and that includes references to incorrect spelling, grammar, and so on. Second, the child may request that his or her journal be private, which must be respected. The third is that when the child invites the adult to read his or her journal, the nature of feedback that the adult gives is more in line with the kinds of reflective responses suggested above and in chapter 7—in other words, responses that ask the child to think and consider further what she or he has written. Fourth, the responses made by the adult are never extensive, consisting instead of just a few words to indicate that the adult has read and is reflecting on what the child has written, and appreciates the child's ideas.

It has been said that "thinking in writing" helps one to clarify his and her thoughts. For that reason alone, journaling is addictive. But it also provides an opportunity to decompress, to unload feelings and thoughts that might be bottled up in one's mind. Some of the most creative minds of the last centuries have used journals to record their experiences, and the notes they left behind serve to not only provide us with glimpses into their thinking but also give us a record of who they were, what they did, what they hoped, and what they dreamed, making our historical record of them more complete. Of course, the more one writes, the more accomplished one becomes, and writing becomes a natural part of who one is.

It has been suggested above that for the purposes of examining moral issues, children's journals can have two focuses. One is open-ended: Children may write whatever comes to mind and for however long they wish to express their thoughts and ideas. The other is in response to prompts—topics suggested by the adult that have moral dimensions. A few ideas for these prompts are found in chapter 5, but these should not be exclusive. There will be issues that arise in class and in the lives of children outside of class, as well as in the neighborhood, the community, the town, the city, the world. And any of these, chosen with an eye and ear to what is appropriate to children's developmental ages, are grist for the mill of journaling.

Teachers who have used journaling with children in the past have often expressed their amazement at the wisdom and the maturity found in even the youngest children who are writing in their journals. So when teachers open this venue to children, they can be expected to be surprised and delighted—and privileged, when they become partners to children's inner worlds.

Many suggestions have been made in this chapter that would enable children to put moral behavior into action. These include outreach projects in which children make singular contributions to the health and welfare of others and to their communities. Follow-up discussions to those outreach projects are also suggested as a means of giving children a chance to extract deeper meanings from their experiences. A prototype of such a discussion is offered as an example of how this may be carried out. While this chapter is likely to be more relevant to teachers, parents interested in outreach experiences for their children may also find ideas that are equally relevant to home use.

Whatever the venue—school or home—outreach activities can provide fulfilling and satisfying opportunities for children to see the benefits of moral behavior not only for others but for themselves as well.

SEVEN

Discussion Strategies to Examine Moral Issues

Mastering the discussion strategies that promote children's thinking, that are respectful in allowing children their own choices, that are nonjudgmental even in the face of contrary points of view, and that ensure that the children feel safe about venturing their ideas is a skill as finely tuned as a 500-year-old violin. Alas, such skill is not innate, nor does it come by wishful thinking. It develops with an understanding of what the strategies involve as well as how they are used. And like other skills, it is perfected with practice and reflection on practice. Most important in such skill development is the parent or teacher's nondefensive awareness of what, exactly, is coming out of his or her mouth.

One of the better ways of learning these interactive strategies is by watching and studying a master of the craft. Given that such training exemplars may be in short supply in one's own neighborhood, some alternate options are available. This is the onus of this chapter—that is, to make clear the what and the how of using "discussion teaching" techniques with young children.

LEARNING DISCUSSION SKILLS BY OBSERVING THE "HOW" IN ACTION

The following prototypical examples demonstrate how a teacher or parent uses selected interactive skills in drawing out and responding to children's ideas on moral issues. When reviewing the examples, it is important to observe how the discussion leader

   a. listens, attends and apprehends the child's statement;
   b. makes sense of what the child is saying;

c. selects, from a variety of options, the type of response to be made, with appreciation that different responses have different cognitive and affective effects;
d. uses questions that put a child's idea under more rigorous examination;
e. uses questions that promote cognitive dissonance;
f. refrains from making moral judgments in the discussion leader's responses;
g. shows respect for the child and the child's beliefs in every response; and
h. ends the discussion without closure; there should be no resolution at the end of each scenario so that the child/children may continue to process the issues after the discussion has concluded.

Note, as well, that the shape of the discussion is A (adult)-C (child): A-C, A-C. Unlike other classroom discussions where students talk with each other, these interactions do not have that shape. There is no A-C1-C2-C3-C4-A, and that is because this is not a dialogue among students but rather a means for the teacher or parent to reach into the mind of the child and work with the child's ideas—to clarify, to seek affirmation, to question.

All of the above represent the primary conditions that make these interactive discussions effective. If one or more of them is violated, there is a danger that the discussion may fail to be productive. For a more in-depth study of interaction skills, the reader is referred to *The Art of Interactive Teaching: Listening, Responding, Questioning* (Wassermann, 2017).

Scene A: The Importance of Being First

A group of six-year old children has been invited to talk to the teacher about why it is so important to them to be first in line. When the teacher calls for the class to line up to go out for recess or lunch, there is often a pushing and a shoving so that someone can beat the others to get to the head of the line. Why is this important? What does it mean to be first in line?

> Teacher: There's something that has been troubling me and I wonder if any of you can explain it. Every day, when we are lining up to go out to recess or lunch, I notice that many of you are so eager to get to be first in line that you race to the door, trying to beat out all the others. And I'm wondering why it is so important for you to be first. Can anyone help me out here?
>
> *At first, there is a long silence. The teacher waits and waits.*
>
> Benny: I just like to be first. That's all.

Teacher: You want to be first, Benny. That's very important to you.

Benny: Yeah. I want to be first. I like to be first.

Teacher: That's why you race to the front of the line. You like to be first.

Benny: Yeah.

Teacher: I wonder where you got that idea, Benny, that being first is important.

Benny: (*Doesn't respond at first. The teacher waits.*) I just like it. That's all.

Teacher: Maybe it's because you think that you are more important if you are first—that it says something about you to be first?

Benny: (*Doesn't respond. Teacher waits.*) I don't know. I'm not sure.

Teacher: Maybe you want to think about it some more. Thanks, Benny. Does anyone else want to say something about being first?

Another silence. Teacher waits.

Silas: I think it's because you just want to get out there fast. Get out to the yard to play.

Teacher: If you are first in line, it means you get out to the yard faster and you can get more time to play.

Silas: Yeah. More time to play.

Teacher: If you are second in line, that would give you less time.

Silas: (*Is quiet for a bit.*) It wouldn't give you that much less time. Just a little bit less.

Teacher: It wouldn't make a big difference if you were second. You'd still have almost the same time to play.

Silas: Yeah. But we just like to be first.

Teacher: There's something more about being first than just having more time to play outside.

Silas: Yeah. I don't know why.

Teacher: It's a puzzle for you Silas. You don't understand why it's important to be first.

Silas: Yeah.

Teacher: Thanks, Silas. Thanks for giving us your ideas. Does anyone else have some ideas to share?

Priscilla: I think it's more the boys who want to race to the front of the line. Lots of girls don't care if they are first or not.

Teacher: You think it's a boys' thing, Priscilla. Girls don't seem to need to be first like the boys do.

Priscilla: Yeah. They push and shove to get to the head of the line, but the girls don't have to do that.

Teacher: Being first in line is more important to the boys than it is to the girls? It's okay for the girls not to be first?

Priscilla: Because boys are more pushy. They think they're better if they are first.

Teacher: Being first, for the boys, means they are better than others. How does this work?

Priscilla: I don't know. It's just the way they are.

Teacher: I wonder if any of the other boys want to say something about what Priscilla has said.

Craig: She's wrong. Not all boys are pushy. Some girls are pushy too.

Teacher: So it's not just a boys' thing. Some girls want to be first too.

Craig: Yeah. It's not everybody. Not every boy and not every girl. But just some of them.

Teacher: Only some girls and some boys want to be first. Not everyone.

Craig: Yeah.

Teacher: Thanks, Craig. I wonder if someone can help me out here. If only some boys and some girls want to get to be first, what explains it? What do you suppose makes them want it? What ideas do you have about that?

Scene B: Throwing Food Around

Mrs. Gordon's seven-year-old daughter Celia has told her mother that some of the children were throwing food around in the lunch room that noon in a food fight. They seemed to be having a lot of fun, but she didn't know if that was right.

Mrs. G: Tell me how the food fight started, Celie.

Celia: (*Softly, as if being pressed for information. And Mrs. G. waits.*) At first, everyone was eating, and it was quiet. Then Mr. Peet [the teacher] left the room, and Brian picked up his apple and threw it at Marcus.

Mrs. G: Brian threw his apple at Marcus.

Celia: Yeah. And it didn't hit Marcus, but Marcus picked it up and threw it back at Brian. And everyone started to laugh.

Mrs. G: So Marcus began to throw food too. He threw the apple back.

Celia: Yeah. And then Joyce did the same thing with her banana. Not the whole banana, but just a piece of it that was left on her plate.

Mrs. G: Once Marcus and Brian started throwing their food, Joyce joined them and threw a piece of her banana.

Celia: Yeah. She threw it at Ariel. And Ariel threw it back.

Mrs. G: Once the boys began to throw food around, two girls got into the action as well.

Celia: And then everyone started throwing food. And laughing. There was food everywhere. It was a mess.

Mrs. G: Maybe it was tempting for you to join in the food throwing as well, once everyone had begun to do it.

Celia: (*Reluctantly*) Yeah. I did it too.

Mrs. G: You were not sure it was good. But you wanted to be part of the game.

Celia: Yeah. Everyone was doing it.

Mrs. G: When you tell me about it, you seem to be a little shy about it.

Celia: I don't know.

Mrs. G: You don't know if you are shy about it?

Celia: I wanted to be part of it. But I don't know if it was right to do it.

Mrs. G: You were not sure. You wanted to join the group, but you were not sure that throwing food was a good idea.

Celia: It was such a mess. There was food all over the floor. And there was all this laughing about it. I don't think it was very funny.

Mrs. G: Throwing food around doesn't seem very funny to you.

Celia: It's okay to throw a ball. But I think it's wrong. Because it made such a mess.

Mrs. G: I'm wondering about something and maybe you can help me here. The boys started throwing the food once the teacher, Mr. Peet, left the room. Do you suppose they would have done that if the teacher was there?

Celia: No, they won't do it when the teacher is looking. Because they would get into trouble.

Mrs. G: So if the teacher is watching, they would not throw food. And if the teacher is not watching, they would do it?

Celia: Yeah.

Mrs. G: Some children need to have a teacher around to keep them from doing something that is not good to do?

Celia: Yeah.

Mrs. G: You are thinking a lot now about how you became part of the food-throwing game and are, perhaps, a bit worried that it was not a good thing to do.

Celia: Yeah. It was such a mess. And when Mr. Peet came back, he was furious. And we all got into trouble.

Mrs. G: So there were some consequences for the class because of the food throwing.

Celia: Yeah. We lost recess for a whole week. Some boys didn't care. But I was sorry that we did it.

Mrs. G: If you had it to do again, maybe you wouldn't do it?

Celia: Yeah. Maybe I wouldn't do it.

Mrs. G: I wonder how come some kids need a teacher around to tell them what's the right thing to do, and some kids know that inside themselves? Do you have any ideas about that?

Scene C: Animals Have Feelings Too!

On a class trip to the zoo, some of the first graders were shrieking at the monkeys in the cage and causing them to shriek back and become quite agitated. Some of the children thought this was great fun, without a care for the way it affected the animals. In a class discussion after the trip, the teacher wanted to query why some of the children thought this was a good thing to do.

Teacher: You all had a good time at the zoo, and some of you especially liked watching the monkeys.

Bruno: The zoo was cool! It was fun!

Teacher: You enjoyed yourselves at the zoo.

Bruno: Yeah. Especially the monkeys. They were cool.

Teacher: You liked the monkeys best.

Bruno: Yeah. They were going crazy. It was a lot of fun.

Teacher: You liked the way they were behaving. It looked like a lot of fun to you.

Bruno: Yeah. We made them do those things because we were yelling at them.

Teacher: So yelling at the monkeys made them do silly things.

Bruno: Yeah. (*He laughs and pokes his friend.*)

Teacher: Would anyone else like to say something about the zoo visit or the monkeys?

Charlene: The boys were making fun of the monkeys. They were yelling at them, and the monkeys got scared.

Teacher: You think the monkeys were scared of the boys who were yelling.

Charlene: Yeah. I didn't think it was nice. People should be nice about the way they treat the animals.

Teacher: You think the boys were not respectful of the animals. They might have been frightening them.

Charlene: Yeah. How would they like it to be put in a cage and made fun of?

Teacher: Some children should think about how they treat the animals. We shouldn't harm them. We should be kind to them.

Charlene: Yeah. Be kind to animals.

Jaime: We weren't being mean to them. We were just making fun.

Teacher: There's a difference between being mean and making fun?

Jaime: Yeah. We didn't mean no harm.

Teacher: You didn't want to upset the monkeys. You thought that yelling at them was okay.

Jaime: I don't know if yelling was okay. Maybe we shouldn't yell.

Teacher: You're not sure if yelling at the monkeys was okay or not.

Isaac: I think the yelling just made them a little crazy. They were jumping all over the place, and they were yelling right back at us.

Teacher: You noticed how the monkeys behaved when some of the boys were shrieking at them. They began to jump around, and maybe they felt unsafe because of the yelling?

Isaac: I say the same as Charlene. How would they like it if people were yelling at them? Animals have feelings too.

Teacher: Animals have feelings. They need to be treated kindly?

Isaac: Yeah. Like you wouldn't shriek at your pets. You would be kind to them. So you should be kind to the animals in the zoo too.

Bruno: We didn't mean any harm. We thought it was fun.

Teacher: Isaac and Charlene don't agree with you, Bruno. What do you say about that?

Bruno: They don't know how the monkeys felt. How did they know that? Maybe the monkeys liked it.

Teacher: It's hard to know what the monkeys felt. But you think they might have liked it?

Isaac: You could tell they didn't like it. The way they were jumping around.

Teacher: We have some disagreements here. Some think that animals have feelings and should be treated kindly. Some of you think that you can't tell how the monkeys felt and that they might have liked the way the boys were yelling at them. I wonder how we can decide what's the right way to act with animals.

THE INTERACTIVE DIALOGUE

The three basic responses in a discussion dialogue that centers on moral issues are listening (attending, apprehending), reflecting (saying back, paraphrasing), and questioning. Underlying all of these is the discussion leader's overt demonstration of respect for the child and for what the child is saying.

1. Listening, Attending, Apprehending

The mainstay of an effective interactive dialogue is the way in which the adult demonstrates, in overall behavior as well as in speech, that he or she is listening to what the child is saying. This listening is not just tuning in but involves full and undivided attention (attending) and the ability to discern or decipher what is meant in the statement and its underlying meanings. This includes making observations of the child's overall behavior (apprehending) as he or she is presenting the ideas.

Giving a child undivided attention sends an important message: "I'm with you. I hear you. You are important to me. What you say is important for me to understand." This is the very essence of what makes an interactive dialogue effective.

Sitting close, making eye contact, and giving the child the adult's full attention enables the adult to concentrate fully on what the child is saying and the behavior that accompanies the statement.

While this skill is not observable in the scenarios above, the way the adult responds to each child throughout the dialogue demonstrates, implicitly, how well the adult is attending to what each child is saying.

2. Reflecting

When the discussion leader is tuned in to what the child is saying, it becomes easier to respond reflectively—that is, to play back what the child has said in either a direct repetition or in a paraphrased statement. Either of these reflective statements enables the child to "see and hear" the statement again—in other words, "This is what you said. Is this what you meant to say?" While on the surface, the reflective response may seem simplistic, it is probably true that very few children (and perhaps even adults) have had an opportunity to hear themselves "played back" to get a more conscious appreciation of what they have said.

The power of these reflective responses is that they allow the child to become more consciously aware of his or her thoughts, ideas, and values. They are no longer just words that are tossed off, never to be considered as having value. The statements now become working material for additional explorations and examinations. The child is responsible for taking ownership of what he or she has said. This is no small benefit.

The end result, after time, of course, is that children become more tuned in to what they are saying and what they are thinking, knowing that what they say will not be taken lightly. It places on them the burden of thinking before speaking and being more cognizant of what they are saying before speaking. In other words, they learn to put their minds into gear before they put their mouths into action.

In the three scenarios, the discussion leader uses several different forms of reflective responses: repetition, an accurate paraphrase, and a slightly torqued paraphrase. Their effect is seen in the way the children use those reflective responses in furthering their own thinking and their own positions on the issue. The process is necessarily slow; the discussion leader does not force a resolution of the issue but allows the ideas to percolate over time.

3. Questioning

In the scenarios above, it is clear that the adult uses questions less frequently than reflective responses. This is a "tell"—while on the surface it would seem that questions have more power to unlock the deeper meanings and get at the core issues than reflections have, the opposite is, in fact, true. Too many questions in too rapid-fire an assault become more of a cross-examination than a thoughtful dialogue. So a good rule of thumb is to use questions sparingly and with an appreciation that they may have the consequence of putting a child on the spot.

Questions are, after all, intrusive. While on the one hand they have power to unlock, they also have the power to intimidate. Much more can be gained, in the long run, from the wise and careful use of reflective responses.

Understanding the different kinds of questions will help guide the intrepid adult as he or she attempts an effective interactive dialogue with children. For example, there are two categories of questions. One category calls for children to think more about the issues being discussed. This category includes questions that:

- Call for observing (What observations have you made about the way the artist uses shapes in that painting?);
- Call for comparing (What differences do you see in those two events? What are some similarities?);
- Call for classifying (How would you group those items?); and
- Call for hypothesizing (What theories do you have about how that works? How do you explain it?)

A second, more challenging category, extends the child's thinking into new territory. These questions ask children to:

- make evaluations,
- interpret data, and
- apply principles to new situations.

This latter category may be less appropriate for the primary age group. For a more detailed description of types of questions and their power to challenge, the reader is referred to *Teaching for Thinking Today: Theory, Strategies and Activities for the K-8 Classroom* (Wassermann, 2009).

The types of questions in the two categories mentioned above are those that may be called productive, in the sense that they are stimulants to deeper and more productive thinking about important issues and events. There are also questions that may be called nonproductive, and these should be avoided. They are nonproductive not only in the sense that they do not enable deeper thought about issues but also because they may effectively shut down students' willingness to venture their ideas.

Among nonproductive questions are "stupid" questions, which neither attend to the child's idea nor are sensitive to the feelings being expressed. For example:

Student: Animals have feelings. They should be treated with respect.

Adult: What kind of pet do you have?

Some questions are too complex. For example:

Student: Animals have feelings. They should be treated with respect.

Adult: Do you think that's in their DNA?

Some questions are deliberately meant to show students up. For example:

Student: I think it's a boys' thing. I think boys like to be first more than girls.

Adult: Wherever did you get *that* idea?

And some questions are laced with sarcasm and meant to humiliate. For example:

Student: It's the Mississippi. That's the longest river.

Teacher: Come on, Brian. Everyone knows it's the Nile.

It should also be noted that the wait time between an adult's question and a child's response needs to be respected, giving the child the time he or she needs to think about an appropriate response. Good ideas don't necessarily come on demand; they need time to be created and formed in the mind before they are given voice. A more effective interactive dialogue is one that respects the wait time between question and response.

What cannot be easily discerned in the scenarios presented above is the nonjudgmental tone of voice of the adult as he or she questions or reflects what a child has said. This is one more essential ingredient of the interactive dialogue. Once the teacher or parent introduces a judgmental tone of voice in a response or in observable behavior, the child immediately grasps the fact that there is no freedom of choice here but only an implicit demand to give the adult what he or she wants. This becomes not a dialogue to tap into children's own thinking but only a ruse to twist the child's thinking toward what the adult considers appropriate or right. In other words, it's a useless exercise.

What can be discerned is the absence of verbal expressions of judgment, such as "good" and "that's an interesting idea." Instead, the adult offers appreciation for the child's contribution: "Thank you, Bruno." There is a world of difference in result between judgment and appreciation.

One final observation about the scenarios is the absence of closure at the end of each of the dialogues. This, too, is an important aspect of these interactive exchanges, since leaving the issues "in suspension" is an inducement for the children to think further—once they have left the discussion—and it sets up the cognitive dissonance that creates the need for the child to ponder the issues. The data from other interactive group work suggest that students continue to think and mull over the issues often long after the dialogue has terminated. In fact, as one student once said, "You remember that film that we were discussing last year in class? I'm still thinking about those issues!"

THE TEACHER/PARENT IN THE PROCESS

The interactive strategies in this chapter form a template for learning what are, likely, high-level professional skills. No one said it was easy. But there are paths to mastery of the skills as well as impediments to the successful acquisition of them.

The first step is awareness of the different kinds of responses and their effects on student thinking and behavior.

The second is the ongoing use of these skills in one-to-one and small-group discussions—that is, reflection in action.

The third is the essential ingredient of nondefensive awareness of self in the process—that is, to be able to hear, without bias, what is coming out of one's mouth.

NONDEFENSIVE AWARENESS OF SELF

A woman was talking to her friend about the dinner she had at her daughter-in-law's house, describing all the faults she found in the meal. The soup was not hot; the meat was not well done; the dessert was too rich; the plates were not warmed; and so on and so forth. When her friend told her she was being excessively judgmental, she snapped back, "I'm not judgmental." It takes an open mind and a nondefensive attitude to be able to own one's beliefs, attitudes, and statements.

Defensiveness, as Rogers (1961) described it back in the early days of client-centered therapeutic work, is "part of the organism's response to experiences which are perceived or anticipated as threatening, as incongruent with the individual's existing picture of himself, or of himself in relationship to the world."

When our sense of self is threatened, we tend to neutralize the threat by distorting the reality of the situation, or by denying it—as the woman did in the above conversation. To own up to her critical judgments would damage her view of herself as thoughtful, kind, good-hearted, generous, and caring. That is a harsh reality for anyone. We would much rather think of ourselves in a more positive frame than to see ourselves as we really may be. It takes a brave, courageous, and very open personality to see oneself as he or she truly is in relation to others and to the world.

This is a vitally important aspect of the adult's work in the interactive dialogue—becoming more accurately aware of one's statements and their effects on others. Learning to listen to self—learning to appreciate, without defensiveness, the effect of one's statements on a child—is a high-level professional task. It requires an openness to our real selves and a willingness to learn to become more like the person we hoped we were.

For the woman complaining about her daughter-in-law, it would mean that she would have to give up any pretense that she is kind, caring, and thoughtful and accept that she is sometimes harsh in her judgments about others. This may be a cruel lesson, but it cannot be evaded if the work to achieve mastery in an interactive dialogue is to proceed.

This question remains: How is this achieved without excessive blows to the ego?

One way—and this may be terrifying—is to practice while videorecording oneself, so that one can watch and listen, after the fact, and make a mental note of any defensiveness that may be creeping, uninvited, into the dialogue. This strategy is not for the fainthearted; but it does provide a good appreciation of how one is actually responding. Watching and listening to oneself is a daunting but very helpful device in seeing, appreciating, and eventually unloading defensive behavior.

Another way is to invite a colleague or friend to listen and watch during a practice session with a child or group of children, and perhaps even to make an accurate transcript of the dialogue. This can be reviewed post hoc and examined for evidence of lack of awareness of how one is actually responding.

In either case, the onus remains on the adult involved in the learning process to note how and where and why his or her responses and behavior falls far from the hoped-for, more effective behavior, to appreciate these insights without defense, and to identify some strategies for correction.

Listening to oneself in the interactive dialogue—becoming more open to oneself in the process—is where the trial steps lead eventually, and it is not different from listening to oneself playing a Mozart sonata. If one cannot begin to hear and appreciate the wrong notes and set up strategies so that those difficult passages become more accessible in future practice sessions, then all hope is lost for making beautiful music.

In the end, it's helpful to remember the advice of Paul Winchell (1954) to budding ventriloquists:

> Don't rush.
> Don't get impatient.
> Don't get discouraged.
> Don't ever give up.

EIGHT
Even Children Can Make a Difference

Morality is not just any old topic in philosophy but is close to our conception of the meaning of life. Moral goodness is what gives each of us the sense that we are worthy human beings. We seek it in our friends and mates, nurture it in our children, advance it in our politics, and justify it with our religions. A disregard for morality is blamed for everyday sins and history's worst atrocities.

There are numerous reasons for people to forsake their morality. The pursuit of financial gain is one compelling force. When push comes to shove, how many among us would eschew profit in favor of what is best for the environment, for health, for the economy, or for the community? The news is full of reports of people in leadership positions whose sense of "the right thing to do" is eclipsed by greed, whose main occupation is recklessly serving themselves with larger and larger profits to the detriment of or at the expense of others.

The pursuit of power and status is another. In order to curry favor with those in power positions, some morally challenged people will disregard what they claim to believe in so that they may rise in an organizational hierarchy. Seeking to advance their careers at the expense of their colleagues by gaming the system, they butter up the boss with bogus flattery in order to ingratiate themselves and gain favor. What matters is not what they know is right; what matters is personal advancement. One word to describe them is *sycophants*. We see them for what they are and despise them.

The need to win is another reason. The expression "It's not enough for me to win; I need to see others fail" is testament to how morality breaks down when the need for success trumps all other human considerations. In one famous example, the ice skater Nancy Kerrigan suffered a broken knee when she was attacked by the ex-husband of her rival so that she would not be able to compete in the Winter Olympics.

Cheating, selfishness, indifference, and greed are all manifestations of needs to put self-interests above the moral issue of "what's the right thing to do." And there are plenty of examples in 21st-century life to give testament to such moral lapses. At the very extreme end of this behavior is what has been called bottomless moral depravity.

Organized religion is one way that societies have attempted to govern the moral behavior of their citizens. Laws put in place by towns, cities, states, and nations are another way in which societies attempt to regulate behavior and keep the populace from committing not only felonies but even small indiscretions like littering and jaywalking. However, even organized religion and civic laws do not altogether prevent immoral behavior. When no one is looking, there is a temptation for some of us to disregard what is "right" and follow the path of least resistance to get ahead, to win, to profit, to gain status and power.

The big idea of this book is to promote a sense of morality in young children, a sense of right and wrong that will guide their lives—that is, guide them to do the right thing when no one is looking—when the church, police, parent, or teacher is not in sight—because that, in itself, is the right thing to do.

Literature provides us with icons that have endured through the ages, characters that we admire because they are moral. They behave in ways that are beacons for us. Children who stood in line for hours to buy the Harry Potter books when they were newly released likely did so because he has been such a hero to them. The original Sherlock Holmes, a character who did not know the word *compromise*, demonstrated his morality in every case he solved. There's a good reason that he remains a star more than a hundred years after his appearance in the Conan Doyle stories. Comic book characters like Spider-Man, the Green Lantern, Superman, and Batman have inspired youth to do good on behalf of others, without concern for self. History and literature provide us with many examples of moral behavior, and they surely provide examples of what children can aspire to.

CHILDREN WHO MAKE A DIFFERENCE

Singular among such iconic figures are three children who, on their own initiative, took action that even adults considered truly astonishing. One of them is the Canadian Craig Kielburger. When Craig was in grade 7, he saw a story in the local newspaper about a murdered 12-year-old Pakistani boy who had been forced into labor in a carpet factory. Kielburger's outrage at this event ignited his interest in child slavery, and he began to gather as much data as he could about child labor worldwide. He was able to interest some of his classmates to help him, and together they formed a group called Kids Can Free the Children. They collected 3,000 signatures on a petition that they sent to the prime minister of India, calling for the release of imprisoned child laborers.

Kielburger, all of 11 years old, became an international hero because of his work in bringing worldwide attention to the notorious practice of using children as indentured laborers in developing countries. Now an adult, Kielburger continues his work and travels around the world espousing his cause. More about Craig Kielburger can be found in a collection of newspaper and magazine articles as well as in his own writings, such as *Free the Children, Me to We,* and *Take Action.* See also https://en.wikipedia.org/wiki/Craig_Kielburger#References.

Craig has been honored by his country and the world, having received the Nelson Mandela Human Rights Award, the Action Canada Fellowship, the Medal of Meritorious Service, and the Queen Elizabeth II Diamond Jubilee Medal, among others. A secondary school in Ontario has been named after him.

Another heroic young boy, Iqbai Masih, also played an important role in bringing international awareness to the scandalous issue of child labor. Iqbai, at age four, was put to work in a carpet weaving factory, to pay off his family's debts. In the factory where he worked for 12 hours a day, he and other children were bound with chains to the carpet looms to prevent their escape. When he was 12, Iqbai escaped and went to the police, but they returned him to the factory. When he escaped a second time, he was able to attend a school for former slaves (Bonded Labour Liberation Front) to complete his education. His work was responsible for freeing more than 3,000 Pakistani children who had been indentured as slave laborers.

Iqbai also become famous worldwide, as he toured making speeches against child labor and encouraged others to join the fight to eliminate child slavery. He paid the price of his life. Iqbai was murdered in 1995; it was suspected that he was killed by those who had been violently opposed to his campaigns.

The third iconic child whose actions have helped to make the world a better place for other children—and women—is Malala Yousafzai, an activist for girls' rights to education. She came from a country where women had few rights and were prohibited from attending school. Her work brought attention to the rights of women to an education in Muslim countries. Malala survived an assassination attempt and went on to become one of the recipients of the Nobel Peace Prize in 2014.

It is not suggested that children put their lives at risk to stand up for a particular moral issue. It is, however, suggested that even children have strong beliefs and that even children who take a moral stand can make a difference. In other words, we should never underestimate young children for who they are and what they can do.

CONCLUSION

That we not underestimate the moral sense of our young children is the hope of teachers and parents, and the materials and strategies offered in this book make a small claim to aid and abet that hope. The bad news is that they are not guarantees of success for every child. No claim is made that teachers and parents who engage children in these ways will ensure that they grow as moral persons who, without an authority figure standing by, will know, on their own, the right thing to do.

But on the other hand, offering nothing but insistence, admonishment, punishment, and advice has a long and systematic failure rate. And the data do suggest that the use of tools and strategies that place children in positions where they must choose, define their values, think, and consider what is right and good does have a better than good chance of success.

Think of it: If we teachers and parents can exercise our leadership to promote more rational and moral behavior in children, what a difference that can make to the future of the world and to the well-being of us all.

Bibliography

Adam, M. (1992). *Responses of eleventh graders to use of case method of instruction in social studies*. Unpublished master's thesis, Faculty of Education, Simon Fraser University, Burnaby, Canada.
Barger, R. N. (2000). A summary of Lawrence Kohlberg's stages of moral development. http://www.qcc.cuny.edu/SocialSciences/ppecorino/MEDICAL_ETHICS_TEXT/Chapter_2_Ethical_Traditions/Reading-Barger-on-Kohlberg.htm
Bloom, P. (2010, May 9). The moral life of babies. *The New York Times Magazine*.
Bok, D. (2008). *Our underachieving colleges*. Cambridge, MA: Harvard University Press.
Brooks, D. (2010, July 23). The moral naturalists. *The New York Times*.
Burke, J. L. (2018). *Robicheaux*. New York, NY: Simon & Schuster.
Chandler, M. J., Greenspan, S., & Barenboim, C. (1973). Judgments of intentionality in response to videotaped and verbally presented moral dilemmas: The medium is the message. *Child Development, 44*, 315–320.
Christensen, R. C., Garvin, D., & Sweet, A. (1991). *Education for judgment: The artistry of discussion leadership*. Boston, MA: Harvard Business School Press.
Dawkins, R. (1976). *The selfish gene*. New York, NY: Oxford University Press.
Ewing, D. W. (1990). *Inside the Harvard Business School*. New York, NY: Random House.
Festinger, L. (1957). *A theory of cognitive dissonance*. Evanston, IL: Row, Peterson and Co.
Gilligan, C. (1982). *In a different voice*. Boston, MA: Harvard University Press.
Glasser, W. (1985). *Control theory in the classroom*. New York, NY: Harper & Row.
Gordon, M. (2005). *Roots of empathy: Changing the world child by child*. Toronto, Canada: Thomas Allen.
The HBS Case Method. (n.d.). Retrieved from https://www.hbs.edu/mba/academic-experience/Pages/the-hbs-case-method.aspx
Hood, E. (1994). *The Hockey Card*. Burnaby, BC: Simon Fraser University Faculty of Education.
Kohlberg, L. (1981). *The philosophy of moral development: moral stages and the idea of justice* (Vol. 1). New York, NY: Harper & Row.
Lickona, T. (1992). *Educating for character*. New York, NY: Bantam Trade Paperbacks.
Lickona, T., Schaps, E., & Lewis, C. (2006). Eleven principles of effective character education: A framework for success. *Journal of Moral Education, 25*(1).
Lockwood, A. L., & Harris, D. E. 1985. *Reasoning with democratic values: Ethical problems in united states history*. New York, NY: Teachers College Press.
Logan, F., & Mayer, R. E. (2013, October). The relative benefits of learning by teaching and teaching expectancy. *Contemporary Educational Psychology, 38*(4), 281–288.
Macklin, R. (1987). *Mortal choices*. Boston, MA: Houghton Mifflin.
Marin, P. (1981, November). Living in moral pain. *Psychology Today*.
Peters, R. S. & Hirst, P. H. (1970). *The logic of education*. London, England: Routledge and Kegan Paul.
Phelan, H. (2018, October 28). Writing in a journal can help. *The New York Times*.
Piaget, J. (1965). *The moral judgment of the child*. London, England: Free Press.
Pinker, S. (2008, January 13). The moral instinct. *The New York Times*.
Press, E. (2018, June 17). The wounds of the drone warrior. *The New York Times Magazine*.
Pugh, G. (1977). *The biological origin of human values*. New York, NY: Basic Books.

Raths, L. E., Harmin, M., & Simon, S. B. (1966; 1978). *Values and teaching*. Columbus, OH: Charles Merrill.

Rogers, C. (1961). *On becoming a person*. Boston, MA: Houghton Mifflin.

Rojas, R., & Mueller, B. (2015, September 15). Defiant Baruch fraternity pledge fought back in fatal hazing. *The New York Times*.

Smetana, J., & Killan, M. (2013). *Handbook of moral development* (2nd ed.). New York, NY: Psychology Press.

Stixrud, W., & Johnson, N. (2018). *The self-driven child: Giving your kids more control over their lives*. New York, NY: Penguin Random House.

Turiel, E. (2002). *The culture of morality*. Cambridge, England: Cambridge University Press.

Wasik, B. (2008, June). When fewer is more: Small groups in early childhood classrooms. *Early Childhood Education Journal, 35*(6), 515–521.

Wassermann, S. (1989). Children working in groups? It doesn't work! *Childhood Education, 65*(4), 201–205.

Wassermann, S. (1990). *Serious players in the primary classroom: Empowering children through active learning experiences*. New York, NY: Teachers College Press.

Wassermann, S. (1994). *Introduction to case method teaching: A guide to the galaxy*. New York, NY: Teachers College Press.

Wassermann, S. (2009). *Teaching for thinking today: Theory, strategies and activities for the K-8 classroom*. New York, NY: Teachers College Press.

Wassermann, S. (2017). *The art of interactive teaching: Listening, responding, questioning*. New York, NY: Routledge.

Wassermann, S. & Ivany, J. W. G. (1996). *Teaching elementary science: Who's afraid of spiders?* New York, NY: Teachers College Press.

Waters, A. (1999). *The edible schoolyard: Learning in the real world*. San Francisco, CA: Chronicle Books.

Winchell, P. (1954). *Ventriloquism for fun and profit*. Baltimore, MD: Ottenheimer.

Index

absence of closure, 18, 80
Aesop's Fables (Aesop), 49
The Art of Interactive Teaching (Wassermann), 70

Back to the Cabin (Blades), 50
Bambi, 52–53
Beauty and the Beast, 53
Beaver Steals Fire (Salish and Kootenai Tribes), 50
The Big Orange Splot (Pinkwater), 49
Big Sister and Little Sister (Zolotow), 50
Blades, Ann, 50
Bloom, Paul, 8, 9
Bok, Derek, 3, 17
Brooks, David, ix, 8, 12, 27
A Bug's Life, 52
Burke, James Lee, 23

Campbell, Nicola, 50
character development: Lickona on, 13; "roots of empathy" in, 13; teachers burden of, 12–13
Character Education Partnership, 13
children, vii, 28, 30, 84; adult relationship trust of, 47; animated Disney films as moral issue for, 29, 52–53; belief communication for, 19; choices allowing and respecting scenario of, 15–16; community project choices of, 55; community project suggestions for, 56–62, 68; data examination of, 29–30; empowered, 20; film classics as moral issue for, 53; follow-up question topics for, 47; group member support for, 47; interactive dialogue ownership responsibility of, 78; journaling and, 66–68; "moral dilemmas" books and films and mini-cases of, 24; moral issue examination of, 2; morality literature for, 29, 49–52; moral sense of, 86; nonjudgmental exchanges for, 18; one-year-old morality sense of, 5, 8; own issue prompts for, 47–49; own morality stories of, 29, 46–49; personal dilemmas of, 46–47; "power to" needs met and unmet of, 19–20; responsible decision-making behavior development of, 1–2; socially responsible behavior and, ix; "street tough" V-group scenario of, x; strong beliefs of, 85; values-laden decisions awareness of, ix; values-related examples of, viii
children, difference making of: Kielburger child laborers work as, 84–85; Masih child slavery work as, 85; Yousafzai girls' education rights work as, 85
children's literature, 29, 84; Aesop moral overtones in, 49; caveat about, 49; First Nations literature examples for, 49–50; Library of Congress and Internet use for, 49; moral dilemmas in, 49; resource abundance in, 52; sensitive issue titles in, 50–52
choices, values-related, 55; absence of closure in, 18; adult values disclosure in, 18–19; allowing and respecting scenario of, 15–16; belief communication in, 19; biological origins in, 1, 12; cognitive dissonance in, 18; consequences and reflection in, 1, 16; in decisions, viii, ix; empathy in, 16; fraternity hazing incident and, 16; as fundamental life

act, 12, 17; justice sense in, 16; moral freedom in, 18; nonjudgmental exchanges in, 18; no "right answers" in, 12, 17; "power to" need in, 19–20; religious and cultural values in, 19; "right thing to do" and scenarios in, 1, 11–12
Cinderella, 53
cognitive dissonance, 8, 18, 70, 80
community projects, 2; adequate protection in, 61; adult monitoring in, 55, 56; bake sale, 56; bottom line of, 62; car wash, 56–57; children choices in, 55; Edible Schoolyard Project example in, 59–60; experience meaning extraction example for, 62–66; follow-up discussion focus in, 62, 67–68; "helicopter parenting" regarding, 55; litter clean up, 60–61; moral sense development in, 55; multiple payoffs in, 61; needs identification in, 56; one-on-one tutoring, 30, 61–62; other opportunities for, 62; putting on show, 58; recycling drives, 59; reflection and meaning making in, 62; school-based, 55, 56; school yard garden and benefits, 59–60; suggestions for, 56–62; teacher role in, 55; toys and games collecting and donating, 57; used books collecting, 58; volunteer dog walking, 58; WWII salvage drives in, 57
Control Theory in the Classroom (Glasser), 19

Dahl, Roald, 51
Dawkins, Richard, 6
decisions, 23; children and, ix, 1–2, 30; choices regarding, viii, ix; complex world of, 12; moral and ethical dimensions in, 17; nature and quantity of, vii; options uncertainties of, 12; reflective responses and higher-order questions in, 2; right choice in, viii; teachers and parents, vii, vii–viii; values protection in, ix; values-related examples of, viii; wisdom and sensitivity in, vii
discussion strategies, 21, 27, 62, 67–68, 69–82; A-C shape of, 70; animal feelings example of, 75–77; being first importance example of, 70–73; food throwing example of, 73–75; interactive dialogue in, 77–81; interactive skill development in, 69; leader principles for, 69–70; nondefensive awareness in, 69; primary conditions in, 70
Dumbo, 52
Dyer, Wayne W., 51

Edible Schoolyard Project, 59–60
Eli's Lie-O-Meter (Levins), 52
Ella Enchanted (Levine), 51
empathy, 13, 16
Everyone Matters (Thomas), 51

Families Change (Nelson and Gallagher), 51
Festinger, Leon, 8
First Nations literature, 49–50
Frank, Anne, 22
Frederick (Lionni), 51
Frog and Toad series (Lobel), 49

Gallagher, Mary, 51
Gilligan, Carol, 7
The Giving Tree (Silverstein), 50
Glasser, William, 19
Gordon, Mary, 13
The Great Blueness (Lobel), 51

Hamlet (fictional character), 21
Harris, David, 22
"helicopter parenting", 55
How Full Is Your Bucket? (Rath), 51

interactive dialogue, 69, 77–81; absence of closure in, 80; basic responses in, 77; careful question use in, 78–81; child ownership responsibility in, 78; direct repetition or paraphrased statement in, 78; judgment and appreciation in, 80; listening, attending and apprehending in, 77;

listening to oneself in, 82; nondefensive awareness of self in, 81–82; nonjudgmental tone in, 80; parent/teacher process in, 81; productive and nonproductive questions and examples in, 79–80; question categories in, 79; questioning in, 78–81; reflecting in, 78; reflective response forms for, 78; Rogers's on defensiveness in, 81; statement awareness in, 81; thinking before speaking in, 78; threat neutralization in, 81; undivided attention use in, 77; video recording and self-correction in, 82; wait time respect in, 80; Winchell advice in, 82

journals, 66–68; benefits of, 66; feedback in, 67; judging of, 67; open-ended or prompt use in, 66–67, 67; privacy respect in, 67; teacher observations in, 67; therapeutic process of, 66; thought clarification in, 67
Junie B. Jones Is (Almost) a Flower Girl (Park), 51
justice, 7, 8, 16, 27–28

Kerrigan, Nancy, 83–84
Kids Can Free the Children, 84–85
Kielburger, Craig, 84–85
Killan, M., 9
Kohlberg, Lawrence, 6–7
Kootenai and Salish Tribes, 50
Krauss, Robert, 52

Lambert the Sheepish Lion, 53
Laurence, Margaret, 50
Leo the Late Bloomer (Krauss), 52
Levine, Gail Carson, 51
Levins, Sandra, 52
Library of Congress, 49
Lickona, Thomas, 13
Lionni, Leo, 51
Lobel, Arnold, 49, 51
Lockwood, Alan, 22
Love You Forever (Munsch), 51
Luria Library, Santa Barbara City College, 50

Macklin, Ruth, 22
Mary of Mile 18 (Blades), 50
Masih, Iqbai, 85
Matilda (Dahl), 51
mini-cases, 30, 32–49; bragging and lying incident in, 43–44; bullying incident as, 45–46; chore finishing obligation as, 39–40; crowd following or own way in, 40; elementary forms of, 31; food sharing dilemma as, 35; getting friends as, 38–39; going to school or days off as, 32; as instructional tools, 31; judgment absence in, 31; lending and safe return issue as, 41–42; lie telling in, 37–38; making fun of classmate as, 44–45; new girl and mother appearance in, 45, 45–46; older brother caring for younger brother as, 33; playing tricks as, 42; positive learning outcomes in, 30; prohibited library book borrowing as, 32; secret telling and trust in, 36–37; social issues non-inclusion in, 31; students as decision makers in, 30; taking something forbidden as, 34; teacher and parent permission regarding, 31; teacher group work problem in, 43; teaching with, 30; tell truth or protect feelings as, 34–35; thinking habits creation in, 30; time making when busy as, 41; truth or lie as, 33–34; unjustly accused situation handling in, 35–36; wild animal conflict as, 46
"moral dilemmas", 6, 7, 46, 49; adult further questioning in, 26; adult reflective responses in, 25; adult value statement obligation in, 26–27; Anne Frank example of, 22; child belief statements interaction in, 26; children's books and films and mini-cases in, 24; child state of ambiguity in, 26; critical reflection in, 23; data examination in, 29–30; decisions difference in, 23; ethical examples of, 22–23; Hamlet example of, 21; in history, 22; issue

and data conflicts in, 24; life and death consequences in, 22, 23; main theme and questions in, 29; materials and discussion strategies in, 21; in modern medicine, 22; moral pain result in, 23–24; no "right" answers in, 23; process examination in, 24; questions and responses in, 25; reflection demands in, 24; respectful attention in, 25; self-awareness in, 23; sensitive examples handling in, 29; sensitive judgments in presenting, 24; small-group work value in, 21, 27–28; Thomas More example of, 22; Truman example of, 22

morality (moral development), 28, 55; "active thinking" in, 7; challenges in, 1; children examination of, 2; children's films and, 29, 52–53; children's literature regarding, 29, 49–52; children's own stories about, 29, 46–49; cognitive dissonance relation to, 8; difference examination in, 7; genetic dispositions relationship to, 6; Kohlberg's research and criticisms in, 6–7; literature icons of, 84; mini-cases use in, 29, 30–46; "moral dilemmas" use in, 6, 7; moral pain concept and example in, 9; moral sense theory in, 8–9; need to win break down in, 83–84; one-year-old child scenario about, 5; organized religion governing of, 84; Piaget stages of development and criticisms in, 6; power and status pursuit instead of, 83; principles of, 10; Pugh's theory of, 6; Raths's idea identification in, 8; rudimentary justice sense in, 8; self-interests above, 84; selfishness and altruism biology in, 6; values clarification workshops in, 8; "values theory" in, 7; worthy human beings sense in, 83; young children sense promotion of, 84

moral pain concept, 9, 23–24
moral sense theory, 8–9

More, Sir Thomas, 22
Mortal Choices (Macklin), 22
Mortimer (Munsch), 51
Munsch, Robert, 50, 51

Nelson, Julie, 51
No Excuses! (Dyer), 51
nondefensive awareness, 69, 81–82
nonjudgmental exchanges, 18, 47, 80
no "right answers", 12, 17, 23, 25, 30

Oliver Button Is a Sissy (de Paola), 52
one-on-one tutoring, 30, 61–62

Paola, Tomie de, 52
The Paper Bag Princess (Munsch), 51
parents, 18–19, 47, 55–56, 56, 68; book as resource tool for, 2–3, 13; decisions by, vii–viii; "helicopter parenting", 55; interactive dialogue process of, 81; mini-cases use permission for, 31; moral dilemmas and, 25–26, 26–27; nonjudgmental stance maintenance of, 47; prepared moral ground responsibility of, 17; resource choosing of, 53–54; socially responsible behavior promotion of, 2

Park, Barbara, 51
Pennebaker, James W., 66
Peters, R. S., 7
Pettranella (Waterton), 50
Piaget, Jean, 6
Pinker, Steven, 8–9
Pinkwater, Daniel Manus, 49
Pinocchio, 53
"power to", 19–20
"prepared ground", ix, 8, 10, 12, 16, 17, 27–28
A Promise Is a Promise (Munsch), 50
Pugh, George, 6

Rath, Tom, 51
Raths, Louis, 7–8, 18
reflection, 1, 16, 23, 24, 62, 78
reflective responses, 2, 25, 78
respect, 15, 25, 67, 80

Salish and Kootenai Tribes, 50

A Salmon for Simon (Waterton), 50
The Selfish Gene (Dawkins), 6
Shi-Shi-Etko (Campbell), 50
Silverstein, Shel, 50
Six Darn Cows (Laurence), 50
small-group work, 21; benefits of, 27–28; child morality scale points in, 28; empowerment sense in, 27; "good group habits" chart creation in, 27; idea interchange in, 27; as learned skill, 27; "prepared ground" in, 27–28; whole-class discussion on, 27
Smetana, J., 9
Snow White and the Seven Dwarfs, 53
socially responsible behavior, 10, 13; children and, ix; as necessary educational goal, 2; parents and teachers promotion of, 2

teachers, 18–19, 47, 55–56; book as resource tool for, 2–3, 13; "character development" burden of, 12–13; community projects role of, 55; decisions by, vii–viii; group work problem mini-case of, 43; interactive dialogue process of, 81; journal observations of, 67; mini-cases use permission for, 31; moral dilemmas and, 25–26, 26; nonjudgmental stance maintenance of, 47; prepared moral ground responsibility of, 17; Raths's idea identification for, 7; resource choosing of, 53; socially responsible behavior promotion of, 2; "street tough" V-group scenario of, x; values-related decision examples by, viii
Teaching for Thinking Today (Wassermann), 79
Thomas, Pat, 51
Too Small (Blades), 50
Truman, Harry, 22
Turiel, E., 9

Values and Teaching (Raths), 8
"values theory", 7
Van Der Wey, Dolores, 49

Walt Disney Company, 52, 53
Wassermann, Selma, 70, 79
Waters, Alice, 59–60
Waterton, Betty, 50
Wells, Rosemary, 52
Winchell, Paul, 82

Yoko (Wells), 52
Yousafzai, Malala, 85

Zola, Meguido, 49
Zolotow, Charlotte, 50

About the Author

Selma Wassermann is a professor emerita in the Faculty of Education at Simon Fraser University, Vancouver, Canada. Her books include *Teaching in the Age of Disinformation: Don't Confuse Me with the Data, My Mind Is Made Up!*; *The Art of Interactive Teaching*; *Teaching for Thinking Today: Theory, Strategies and Activities for the Classroom*; *Serious Players in the Primary Classroom*; *The New Teaching Elementary Science*; *This Teaching Life*; and *The Long Distance Grandmother*.

www.ingramcontent.com/pod-product-compliance
Lightning Source LLC
Chambersburg PA
CBHW030147240426
43672CB00005B/309